ECONOMICS
with justice

PART 2
Ideas

Ideas

Why we think the way we think

> "The ideas of economists and political philosophers, both when they are right and when they are wrong, are more powerful than is commonly understood. Indeed the world is ruled by little else."
>
> -- John Maynard Keynes

Prosperity and happiness for all continue to evade us, despite our best endeavours. Is it our thinking that is getting in the way?

This ten week course examines some of the key ideas that powerfully influence the way we think and the way we relate to others in the world economic community.

Through challenging presentations and lively discussion, explore the possibility of stepping free of them to appreciate a greater sense of justice for humanity.

Synopsis

1: What rules us? - the origins of economic science

2: What do we own? - private property by Locke and Blackstone

3: What motivates us and who benefits? - the "invisible hand" of Adam Smith

4: Is there enough for everyone? - doubts by Ricardo and Malthus

5: Can we replace the market? – utilitarian Bentham and radical Marx

6: What about social needs? - social developments, land enclosure and Henry George

7: How do we value and set a price? - neo-classical Marshall and the theory of the firm

8: What is the last resort? – 20th century catastrophe and Keynes

9: Freedom from all or freedom for all? - monetarist Friedman or natural law

10: The way forward: Consensus and Economic Justice

To enrol visit www.schooleconomicscience.org by telephone 020 7034 4000 or in person at 11 Mandeville Place Reception.

School of Economic Science, 11 Mandeville Place, London, W1U 3AJ

Supporting local economies:
from Business Rates to Land Value Taxation

Julian Pratt

Henry George Society of Devon

Occasional Paper

Published by

First Published 19th May 2014

ISBN   978-1-291-87918-6

To order a paperback copy go to www.stewardship.ac or www.lulu.com

A free pdf download available from www.stewardship.ac/orders.htm and
http://henrygeorgedevon.wordpress.com/

Acknowledgements. The author would like to thank Alan Gorman for
provoking the introductory 'context' piece. For 'taking Mirrlees
forward' he would like to thank Rosemary Field, Alan Gorman, Greg
McGill, Justin Robbins, Tony Vickers, Dave Wetzel and Jonty Williams
for conversations, comments and suggestions. Particular thanks are
due to the constructive and detailed comments of an anonymous
reviewer. Any remaining errors and omissions are the author's alone.

www.stewardship.ac

Henry George Society of Devon

CONTENTS

Context for the business rates proposal

In the summer of 2013 Jonty Williams and I visited the constituency surgery of the Conservative MP for Totnes, Dr Sarah Wollaston, to talk about Land Value Taxation. She raised several thoughtful challenges to our proposal, and made clear that she would not lobby for this change to take place as it is is not her specialist area of expertise. However she agreed to look at a briefing paper, and send it to David Gauke MP, Exchequer Secretary to the Treasury.

In concluding that in Treasury's view a Land Value Tax is not a tenable proposal at this time, David Gauke's response [David Gauke 2014], in summary, was that the proposal would:

- be a significant tax reform
- take a number of years to deliver
- be complex to introduce and costly to administer
- change the current distribution of tax on non-domestic property and on businesses, creating winners and losers
- be likely to shift the tax burden from intensive high-rise buildings to agricultural land.

We were disappointed that, even if the proposal is considered to be politically unacceptable, this response failed to acknowledge either its economic benefits or indeed that each of these points is addressed in the paper.

The paper, *Taking Mirrlees forward: Replacing National Non-Domestic (Business) Rates by Land Value Taxation*, was published in November 2013 by the Henry George Society of Devon and is reprinted below. Colleagues in the Henry George Society of Devon are broadly supportive of the proposal, but have raised some questions:

Q. So you have written a proposal to introduce Land Value Taxation, but only for non-domestic land. Surely the most urgent issues are housing and the environment. Land Value Taxation could make housing more affordable and reduce environmental degradation, so why focus on increasing business profitability and competitiveness?

A. Well, the proposal would make a big difference to housing. At the moment no business rates are payable on derelict or undeveloped land, even when there is planning permission for dwellings, or on properties that are unable to command a rent because of their poor condition. If a tax on the value of land were to replace business rates all this land would be less attractive to hold out of use, and there would be a real stimulus to develop it for housing as well as for business use.

But to be honest it was a pragmatic decision to focus on non-domestic land. When Sarah Wollaston asked us to outline our proposal, this just seemed the natural place to start – particularly as the Conservatives describe themselves as natural supporters of business, and here is a proposal to remove a tax that damages business. There are several reasons, though, which underlie the decision.

One is that, although Land Value Taxation was out of favour during the last half of the twentieth century, there are now many orthodox economists who support its introduction. I first started thinking about a reform that was limited to the business rates when I read the Mirrlees review. Here the Nobel prizewinner for his work on optimal taxation was recommending changes to the British tax system that include replacing the unsatisfactory system of business rates with Land Value Taxation.

Another reason for focusing on business rates is that there should be much more support, and less opposition, for a proposal to tax business land than there would be for residential land. Taxing business land doesn't affect homeowners. It doesn't affect businesses that rent their property from a landlord. Owners of well-developed business land profit from it, whether they are landlords or owner-occupiers. And all owners of business land would understand that, for every pound taken in Land Value Tax, the business community as a whole would gain by a pound taken off other business taxes – taxes that are damaging to business because they discourage employment, investment, adding value and making a profit.

There are practical advantages in taking forward a proposal as radical as Land Value Taxation in parts. If it could demonstrate benefits when applied to non-domestic land it would have more support, and there would be more experience with the practical details, than there is now. This would provide a stronger base of support for introducing Land Value Taxation for all land. The practical challenges of introducing Land Value Taxation are not so much those of introducing the tax itself, but of unravelling the current system of taxes. And unravelling business taxes on their own is a simpler proposition than making changes to personal taxes and benefits.

Q. Isn't there is a danger that piecemeal introduction of Land Value Taxation could lead to a tax system that is just as fragmented and cobbled-together as the present one?

A. I think there are two steps to think about if you want to introduce Land Value Taxation. The first is 'how would it work in an ideal world?' And the second is 'how could we make the transition to that ideal world from where we are now?' The ideal is fairly straightforward to describe, but transition would be more complicated.

The general principle of Land Value Taxation is that everyone is entitled to an equal share of the wealth of the natural world. One method of sharing the revenue from a Land Value Tax is for the government of the day to use it to provide public goods like infrastructure, education and so on. The other is to distribute it as a cash income to each person, equally, as a small private income. The practical question is: 'as you start to make the transition, what do you use the revenue for?' The obvious answer would seem to be to use the revenue to replace the taxes on jobs, enterprise and adding value that currently do so much damage to the economy. But it's not quite that simple. I think that transition falls naturally into three areas – domestic (housing) land, non-domestic (business) land and the environment. And that transition should follow a rather different path for each.

As far as environmental charges and taxes are concerned, the temptation is for government to use them to raise new revenue – people are probably right to talk about them as 'stealth taxes'. I think that we should pool all the revenue from (increases in) environmental charges and taxes, and distribute it on an equal per capita basis as an Environmental Dividend. This keeps the deterrent effect of a tax on landfill or fuel or whatever, as you have to pay for your use of the environment. But if you use less than an equal per capita share of that resource you will receive more income as Environmental Dividend than you pay as tax or duty – and if you use more than your share you are out of pocket. By and large this transfers wealth from the rich, who are high users, to the poor. But there are some cases where poorer people may pay more in environmental charges and taxes than the rich, for example for heating their home. These costs may be largely outside the control of poorer people, particularly those living in rented accommodation that is poorly insulated, so there has to be additional regulation and funding for home insulation and other environmental protection measures. But an Environmental Dividend would be overwhelmingly progressive, and any associated tax or charge could not be dismissed as a stealth tax. If the revenue was used in this way lots of people would then benefit directly from environmental taxes and charges, and even those who didn't benefit would understand the rationale. This should lead to more support for environmental taxes and charges. Of course this isn't ideal – the sustainable use of non-renewable resources means that resource rents really should be re-invested in maintaining the stock of natural capital, or at least used for something that will be of lasting benefit to future generations. But as a short-term measure it would get us out of our present failure to put a price on environmental damage.

The revenue from a Land Value Tax on business land should be used to replace existing taxes that reduce business profitability, leaving the overall burden of taxation on business unchanged. The impact would be to increase the tax burden on sites that are underused and underdeveloped, particularly empty and derelict land, while reducing the tax on sites where the land is put to good use within the limits permitted by the planning system. This should be beneficial for all owners of well-developed and well-used business land, apart from those who own land that currently gets an exemption or relief from National Non-Domestic (Business) Rates.

That leaves the question of how best to use the revenue from domestic land. The first thing to do is to use it to replace existing property taxes – the highly regressive Council Tax, and Stamp Duty Land Tax as this causes such inefficiencies in the housing market. It might then seem sensible to use it to reduce the burden of Income Tax, as this clearly damages the economy and takes from people what they have earned by their own effort. But there are several reasons not to start here. One is that using the revenue in this way does nothing for the poorest people, particularly those on benefits who are not paying Income Tax. Another is that there is a group of people who would be paying Land Value Tax but who would gain little from a reduction in Income Tax – particularly owner-occupiers who have retired or are working in areas that have gentrified and experienced steep rises in land values. Yet another is that it misses the opportunity to reform the current dysfunctional benefit system, which subjects people to demeaning means-tests and discourages them from getting into work. So once the Council Tax and Stamp Duty Land Tax have gone I would like to see the revenue from domestic land used to replace the current benefit system, gradually, by a Universal Income that everybody would benefit from. This would probably require a time-limited extension of housing benefit to owner-occupiers, funded from the Land Value Tax. Once reform of the benefit system was under way you could move on to replacing other taxes. The priority would be employee's National Insurance contributions and VAT, because both are regressive and damaging to the economy; Income Tax would be one of the last to be removed.

I think that separating out these areas – environment, domestic land and non-domestic land – would create a coherent and transparent reform in which each area could go ahead at its own speed. The great advantage is that the use of the revenue would be completely transparent – environmental charges transferring wealth from high users to low users, and the Land Value Tax on business land used to reduce taxes on business.

Q. All right, lets just focus on this proposal for business land. There are several things that worry me. First of all, won't replacing the National Non-Domestic (Business) Rates by Land Value Taxation just stimulate the economy and exacerbate the excesses of the consumer society and all the environmental problems that economic growth causes?

A. I think we would agree that economic growth in high consumption economies is fundamentally unsustainable because of the damage that it does to the environment. The immediate problem is that, as Tim Jackson accepts in *Prosperity without growth*, other things being equal the natural dynamics of capitalism push it towards either expansion or collapse (Tim Jackson 2009/2011: 64). I'm no believer in trickle-down but when growth stops or slows, as in the recent recession and its aftermath, it is the poor who have borne the brunt – particularly those who have lost their jobs. Economic growth over the last half-century has been the one thing that has made widening income inequalities slightly more tolerable. And public pressure to reduce environmental charges like fuel duty, for example, show how difficult it is to protect the environment when economic growth is slow.

Of course other things do not need to be equal and we should be taking steps that would lead to prosperity without growth – tackling income inequalities, providing security for people's livelihoods, removing the focus on labour productivity, investing in environmental protection and preserving natural capital (Tim Jackson 2009/2011: 141-2).

One of the structural problems in the current economic arrangements is that we choose to distribute the wealth created in our complex and interdependent economy primarily to those who work, who invest, or who own land; with the rest spent grudgingly on public services, pensions and other benefits. So we are driven to do everything that we can to reduce unemployment. Land Value Taxation offers a way to remove this need to prop up growth in order to keep people in work. I've already said that I would like to see public services funded from a Land Value Tax, with the residual revenue distributed as a Universal Income, and the revenue from environmental charges distributed as an Environmental Dividend. These unconditional incomes distribute the wealth that we create in a way that is independent of work and so reduce our dependence on economic growth.

V

So you are right about the danger that this proposal, limited to non-domestic land, could lead to excessive economic growth if it were to be implemented on its own. Ideally I'd like to see the proposal introduced in parallel with charges for the use of the environment; these would be likely to damp down economic growth, particularly growth that damages the environment. And I'd like to see it introduced in parallel with Land Value Tax on domestic land, which would provide the resources for a Universal Income. But even on its own it would be a step in the right direction.

Q. All right, if we see the business rates proposal as part of a wider move towards a full Land Value Tax then I'm happy to go along with it. But there's another set of problems, the impact of the proposal on small businesses. For a start there are already lots of shops around the country that are boarded up or let to charities because business rates are too high. Won't this make the situation worse?

A. Not at all. The main cause of this excessive burden of business rates is the failure to carry out frequent revaluations. Most businesses are still paying rates that reflect the value of market rents before the recession struck. With a bit of political will the existing business rates could be revalued more often. But Land Value Taxation would automatically provide frequent (at least annual) valuations as these are integral to the system.

Q. Doesn't the proposal disadvantage small businesses, though? Big businesses can afford to invest in developing their properties, so they are likely to gain more from the reduction on the tax on buildings than they lose from the increase in the tax on land. But there are lots of small businesses that own their own premises and are only just hanging on. If they have been unable to invest in their buildings, and their site is valuable, they would pay more in Land Value Taxation than they had in National Non-Domestic (Business) Rates.

A. Some sites may be genuinely on the margin of profitability – whatever use they are put to, as permitted by the planning system, they can only just cover their running costs and wages. Any payment of rent and rates would put them out of business. The good news is that the Land Value Tax on these sites would be zero, and as long as no rent was charged even these marginal sites would continue to support some sort of enterprise.

Other sites could be profitable enough to pay some level of rent and/or rates – but if they are boarded up then the rent and rates currently being asked are, taken together, too high. A Land Value Tax would never be more than the occupier was willing to pay in the open market, so a site like this would always be profitable.

But the sites that I think you are talking about are those where somebody else would be prepared to pay more, in rent and rates, than the present occupier (for uses permitted by the planning system). As well as being small in number, I don't think that these are particularly deserving cases. If somebody else is prepared to pay a higher rent, and particularly if they are prepared to invest in the building to make the site more productive, wouldn't that new use generally be better for the local economy as a whole than the persistence of an unproductive business? But I know that might seem hard. I think that, if the community wants to preserve particular types of business use even if they are not particularly profitable, the way to do so is through the planning system.

The people who really lose from this reform are not those whose premises need refurbishment but those who are holding empty and derelict land.

Q. But isn't David Gauke right, that Land Value Tax would shift the tax burden from intensive high-rise buildings to agricultural land?

A. The reason that agricultural land pays no business rates is that it is currently exempt. For the reasons set out in the paper I think that it should be brought back into the system of taxation rather than being subsidised by other businesses, but that this transition needs to be handled carefully.

His substantial point is that there would be a transfer of tax burden from intensively used land, for example supporting high-rise buildings, to relatively undeveloped land. This is only correct if the land is undeveloped because that is the owner's choice. It would transfer the burden from land that is currently being used as intensively as permitted by the planning regulations to land that is being used less intensively than permitted. So there would be no transfer of the tax burden from a high-rise to a low-rise building unless the planning regulations allowed the low-rise site to support a high-rise building. In that case the tax would have the beneficial effect of stimulating the development of the underdeveloped site that the planners want to see developed more intesively.

Q. Well I certainly don't want to favour large businesses and multinationals and see the wealth that we have in the local economy being sucked out. Strengthening the local economy is the rationale behind the Totnes pound, for example.

A. Absolutely. But there is a limit to how much a local initiative can achieve when it is continually undermined by national policy, particularly on taxation.

Q. So how does national taxation undermine the local economy?

A. Most taxation doesn't take into account the significance of geography – of location. Some places are good for business, and rents here are high; other places are not so good and rents are lower. But most conventional taxes are the same wherever the business is located – National Insurance contributions, VAT and Corporation Tax for example. These taxes act as a greater disincentive at the already disadvantaged sites, and may even put these out of business.

Q. I can see that a Land Value Tax could make these businesses on marginal sites more profitable by reducing the burden of other taxes. I can see that in some places that could stimulate those local economies. But that's not what you are proposing – you are suggesting using a Land Value Tax to replace National Non-Domestic (Business) Rates. And these already reflect the value of the land that the business uses.

A. Well, business rates fall on both the value of the land *and* the value of the buildings. The part that falls on the land is, as you say, a form of Land Value Tax. But it is combined with the part that falls on the buildings and other improvements, and this is seriously harmful to business. It penalises building and improving – shops, offices, factories and so on. It may even promote dereliction, as this reduces the tax burden. Stage 1 of this proposal would replace a part-good, part-bad tax (business rates) with a wholly good tax. Stage 2 would reform the whole of business taxation by replacing VAT on refurbishment, employers' National Insurance contributions and eventually Corporation Tax and VAT.

Q. So would it put sites that are currently derelict or underused under pressure to develop?

A. Well its effect on an underused site is to exert a powerful pressure to develop. But there is another factor that partly counterbalances this. Land Value Taxation would release underused land on to the market, and with more land available for development there would be less pressure on each individual site. Land Value Taxation would lead to more uniform development, not to a skyscraper on every plot – even if that were permitted by the planners.

Q. Some sites that are currently described as brownfield development sites have been derelict for so long that they have become important as urban wildlife sanctuaries or as places for recreation. Would these be taxed into use?

A. For these sites it's very much the same as for existing parks, many of which would be valuable development sites but which we decide collectively to protect from development by the planning system. If the planners think these brownfield sites are worth protecting, they can do so.

Q. I don't think you understand the limitations of the planning system. At the moment developers can generously fund endless applications and appeals, and the odds are stacked against a Local Authority that wants to limit development but simply can't afford the legal representation. The planning system would come under a lot of pressure, and need more resources.

A. Absolutely. Land Value Taxation puts planning at the heart of the economic system. Planning would need to be transparent and properly resourced.

Q. What we haven't talked about is that some people are bound to lose from this. You've already mentioned owners of business land that is under-developed – presumably they would have to pay this new tax, and to be able to do so they would have to invest in their property so that it earned them a better rent?

A. Yes, or they could sell it to somebody who would invest in it.

Q. So who would lose then?

A. You have to own non-domestic land to lose from this reform. The land has to be relatively under-developed, or to be paying little or no business rates at present due to the quirks of the system of National Non-Domestic (Business) Rates and its exemptions and reliefs for charities and farmers. There are good reasons for subsidising charities and farmers, but exempting them from business rates is a terrible way of doing so as this distorts land use, leads to its under-use and pushes the burden of taxation on to other owners. So *Taking Mirrlees forward* proposes replacing these exemptions and reliefs with direct subsidies to charities. And it proposes exempting agricultural land from Land Value Taxation for at least 5 years, with the possibility of extension if a case can be made.

Q. I can see that I had better read the fine print, then.

Taking Mirrlees forward:

Replacing National Non-Domestic (Business) Rates by Land Value Taxation

- need, impact and proposal for feasibility study

Henry George Society of Devon

Occasional Paper

November 2013

Executive Summary

'[Land Value Taxation] is such a powerful idea, and one that has been so comprehensively ignored by governments, that the case for a thorough official effort to design a workable solution seems to us to be overwhelming. In particular, significant adjustment costs would be merited if the inefficient and iniquitous system of business rates could be swept away and replaced by an LVT [Land Value Tax]' (James Mirrlees et al 2011: 377).

LVT has been advocated by mainstream economists including Nobel prizewinners for their work on optimal taxation (William Vickrey 1995: 17, James Mirrlees et al 2011: 377), the Organisation for Economic Co-operation and Development (OECD 2010:10), the International Monetary Fund (John Norregaard 2013:16) and the Economist (Economist 2013). A major current economic challenge is to find ways to stimulate the economy without increasing the budget deficit, and the reform described here would achieve this through a revenue-neutral change in the way that taxes on business are raised. This paper sets out the need for change, proposes a two-stage reform, describes its anticipated impact and proposes that Treasury conduct a feasibility study.

Non-Domestic (Business) Rates are not efficient

Business rates have been described as a combination of 'one of the worst taxes – the part that is assessed on real estate improvements... – and one of the best taxes – the tax on land or site value' (William Vickrey 1995: 17). By penalising building, business rates damage the profitability and competitiveness of business and impose a deadweight loss on the economy. They also provide an incentive to under-develop land, and even to demolish viable buildings, to minimise the burden of rates.

Two-stage reform

In Stage 1 of the proposed reform, which follows the main recommendation for business taxation set out in the Mirrlees review (James Mirrlees et al 2011:491), the National Non-Domestic (Business) Rates (NNDR) are replaced by a Land Value Tax (LVT) in a revenue-neutral fashion. Existing exemptions and reliefs from NNDR would either not be carried over (applied) to the LVT (e.g. those for vacant and unused land) or carried over but phased out (e.g. those for agricultural land and charities).

LVT would be levied on the owner of each non-domestic site as a proportion of the annual market rent of the land, assessed on the assumption that the site is put to the highest and best use (Glossary). Two properties (land plus buildings) that currently have the same value, and so are paying the same level of NNDR, may be liable to pay different levels of LVT. A site that is under-developed relative to other similar sites with similar planning conditions, and is used inefficiently, will have a high land value relative to the total value of the property (land plus buildings) and will pay more LVT than it does NNDR. A well-developed site will have a lower land value as a proportion of total value, and pay less LVT than NNDR.

In Stage 2 any future increase in the market rent of non-domestic land is taxed, and the revenue is used in a revenue-neutral way to replace taxes that damage business. This replacement would start by phasing out VAT on the refurbishment of buildings, followed by Stamp Duty Land Tax and then employers' National Insurance Contributions. These would be replaced by LVT at a speed determined by the rate of growth, if any, in land values. 'Stage 2 LVT' is levied at 100% of the increase in market rent of non-domestic land, and so would effectively cap the market value (sale price or capital value) of this land. This would prevent the fluctuations in non-domestic land values that have caused repeated banking failures and recessions around the world (Martin Wolf 2010).

The replacement of NNDR by LVT stimulates the economy in three ways. It cuts taxes on businesses that are using their land efficiently, by broadening the business property tax base to include all non-domestic landowners (not just occupied business premises). It frees up relatively unproductive land for development. And it stimulates development, both because businesses are able to develop their buildings without paying more tax and because government investment in infrastructure such as new rail lines is automatically recovered though an increase in tax revenue that captures the rise in land value caused by the investment.

Summary of anticipated benefits of the reform (Stages 1&2)

Macroeconomic benefit

- more than £3 billion per year stimulus to the economy in Stage 1, increasing in Stage 2

- in Stage 2 business taxes rise automatically in times of rapid economic growth, reducing the magnitude of any boom. They fall automatically in recessions (Page 15), providing a stimulus to business and the economy

- in Stage 2 a cap is effectively placed on the market value of non-domestic land, preventing boom and bust cycles in non-domestic

2

land and the consequent risk to the banking system

Increased business profitability and international competitiveness

- property taxes are reduced for businesses that make efficient use of their land

- property taxes are reduced for businesses operating on marginal land

- the business property tax base is broadened

- businesses benefit from increased infrastructure investment

- in Stage 1 there is a one-off loss in market value for owners of land but a windfall gain for owners of buildings and other improvements. In consequence owners of well-developed land will be rewarded by reduced levels of taxation and increased property values. Owners of poorly-developed land will be encouraged to develop the property to its highest and best use, or to sell it to somebody who will do so

- in Stage 2 a cap is effectively placed on the market value of non-domestic land, reducing the capital costs for future start-up businesses

- in Stage 2 VAT on the refurbishment of buildings, Stamp Duty Land Tax and employers' National Insurance Contributions are reduced, and eventually removed

Regeneration of under-developed areas

- reduced business taxation in (geographically marginal) areas that are currently unattractive will encourage new businesses to locate there, and existing businesses to expand locally

Self-funding infrastructure

- well-conceived infrastructure (e.g. transport, fast broadband) increases the profitability of the businesses that are positively affected, and so the value of their land. This results in higher levels of LVT, which may in turn be used to finance the infrastructure and allow it to become self-funding

- owners are automatically compensated if their environment deteriorates (by the amount that their rent falls)

Reduced tax avoidance and evasion

- reduced vandalisation of potentially viable buildings to avoid NNDR

- reduced evasion of VAT, Stamp Duty Land Tax and National Insurance Contributions in Phase 2

Optimal land use

- reduced incentives to hold land for speculation and land banking

- financial incentives that bring all land into optimal use, increase the supply of land and lower land prices

- no tax penalties for developing or improving buildings

- incentive to ensure that all non-domestic land is in the hands of those who can make best use of it

- efficient use of all land leads to compact development, reduction in urban sprawl with reduced infrastructure costs, less pressure on the green belt and reduction in carbon dioxide emissions.

Feasibility study

LVT warrants a feasibility study by Treasury and this should explore mechanisms for valuation, revaluation, transition and piloting. The major challenge is to agree a way to value land independently of the buildings on it, which is not common practice in the UK. Treasury need to look not just to their usual advisors on valuation (including the Valuation Office Agency, the Royal Institution of Chartered Surveyors and the Institute of Revenues Rating and Valuation) but to those with experience of jurisdictions where LVT is in place and to UK experts such as the Professional Land Reform Group.

Introduction

This paper, intended for Treasury economists, describes a proposal to replace National Non-Domestic (Business) Rates (NNDR) with a Land Value Tax (LVT).

The paper begins by setting out some background information about LVT and NNDR and clarifying that this proposed reform is limited to non-domestic property. This is followed by two sections, describing Stages 1 and 2 of the reform, that highlight the deficiencies of the current regime of business taxes and set out how the reform would address them. After summarising the anticipated benefits of the two stages taken together, the paper sets out the issues that should be considered in a feasibility study.

The reason for dividing the proposed reform into two stages is pragmatic. Stage 1 replaces NNDR with LVT, and would deliver immediate real benefits by stimulating the economy and improving the efficiency of land use. It takes the form of a practical proposal to implement the Mirrlees proposals, except that in order to maintain strict revenue-neutrality vis à vis NNDR it does not include any changes to Stamp Duty Land Tax.

Stage 2 of the reform charts a course for the future of business taxation. It collects any future increases in the market rent of non-domestic land and uses the resulting revenue to reduce existing taxes that damage business, starting with VAT on the refurbishment of buildings and progressing to Stamp Duty Land Tax and employers' National Insurance Contributions. Stage 2 is, therefore, revenue-neutral vis à vis business taxation as a whole.

This proposal for a two-stage reform is just one of many possible ways to replace NNDR and other business taxes with LVT. It is described here not as an attempt to pre-empt other trajectories that have been proposed to achieve the replacement (e.g. Christopher Glover 2013, John Muellbaur 2005, Dave Wetzel 2013), but to provide one illustration of how it could be achieved.

Background

Impact of taxes on rent

Valuation practice makes use of the 'equation theory' (Roger Emeny & Hector Wilks 1984: 187 sect 8.13), which asserts that a tenant is concerned with the total rent and rates that they have to pay for their property, not either one in isolation. This total is determined by the profitability of the business. The consequence is that if NNDR increase then a tenant will not be able to pay as much rent, while if NNDR fall they will be able to pay a higher rent. Although the *liability* to pay NNDR normally falls on the tenant, its *incidence* (the ultimate burden of the tax) falls on the owner.

One piece of supporting evidence for 'equation theory' is provided by the evaluation of the removal of property tax on non-domestic land in the Enterprise Zones of the 1980s. This found that the *'rates concession represents a direct saving to tenants (and owner occupiers) but there is evidence that it is largely offset by higher market rents, which in turn feed through into capital and land values'* (Department of the Environment 1988: 40).

Land Value Taxation

Land Value Taxation is not the same as other forms of land tax such as National Non-Domestic (Business) Rates or betterment levies like the Development Land Tax. A Land Value Tax is an annual tax equal to some proportion of the annual market rent (Glossary) of each plot of land (not including buildings and other improvements), based on its highest and best use.

It is levied on the owner. The market rent should ideally be established directly in the market, but where this is not possible it is assessed as the rent that a valuer can demonstrate that the land would command if it were put to its highest and best use. This is *not* necessarily its current use and *not* necessarily encumbered with the existing buildings, unless these are protected from demolition by listing. The valuation for the purposes of Land Value Tax therefore reflects the optimal use that is legally allowable, physically possible and economically feasible – taking into account any planning conditions and the plans approved by the Local Planning Authority.

Proposal limited to non-domestic land

Land Value Taxation, as an approach to raising public revenue from land, has been applied in only a limited way around the world (Robert Andelson 2000) in spite of its clear advantage as a tax that imposes no deadweight loss on the economy (Julian Pratt 2011: 103) and as a tax with a powerful ethical foundation (Julian Pratt 2011: 96-7). One reason is technical – the perceived difficulty of valuing land separately from buildings. Another is political – the opposition (Coalition for Economic Justice 2012) from owners of domestic (Glossary) properties who have adapted their lifetime spending and investment decisions to the economic distortions created by the current tax-benefit system, and amongst whom some would lose and some would gain if LVT were to be introduced on domestic properties.

For this reason this proposal does *not* relate to properties that are currently used for domestic purposes. Many of those who argue against Land Value Taxation when applied to domestic properties ('taxing people to live in their own homes') would not necessarily oppose its application to non-domestic properties. (A property that is used for both domestic and non-domestic purposes would be treated as two separate properties.)

National Non-Domestic (Business) Rates (NNDR)

NNDR are levied on units of real estate that normally correspond to each separately occupied property. They are intended to reflect the net annual market rent of the whole property (buildings plus land), assuming that it is put to its existing use (Local Government Finance Act 1988, Schedule 6). This is calculated for each property by multiplying its 'rateable value' (assessed by the Valuation Office Agency, an executive agency of Her Majesty's Revenue and Customs) by the non-domestic rates multiplier, or uniform business rate (set by central government at 41.3% for England in 2010).

The main features of NNDR are that:

- the basis of liability is the net annual value, assuming *existing* use, of land *and* buildings. Valuation assumes that buildings cannot be altered structurally and that the site can only be used for its present mode of occupation. The site of a city hall is valued as the site for a municipal building, not as a site that could be used, perhaps at a higher market rent, for shops – even if shops would be permitted by planning regulations

- valuation is based on the 'open market annual rental value' of the property (GOV.UK 2013) but this is derived from the rent of the tenancy from year to year, and assumes that a hypothetical tenancy exists (Owen Connelan 2004:40). So it is based on the existing physical condition and use of the property, not its highest and best use (Coalition for Economic Justice 2013)

- the net annual value is reduced by the amount of any physical obsolescence (structural deterioration) and of any functional obsolescence (for example an ornate city hall would only attract the net annual value of a modern building with equivalent functionality)

- *liability* to pay NNDR generally falls on the occupier not the owner (though it falls on the owner if unoccupied). Imposing NNDR where it was not applied before would reduce rents, because the ability of the occupier to pay a higher rent is limited

- NNDR apply to all non-domestic property; but a complicated and ever-developing set of reliefs and exemptions, both mandatory and discretionary, apply to a range of property uses and users

- No NNDR are payable for derelict and undeveloped land, buildings under construction, and properties that are unable to command a rent because of their poor condition.

Rating law states that a property that does not command a rent cannot be valued for tax purposes, and so is not liable for NNDR. Non-domestic properties that are empty (but useable) became exempt from 1985 to 2008, but this exemption is now limited to three months. A major consequence of the current arrangement, where NNDR are levied on viable properties that are unused, is that the taxpayer has no revenue from which to meet the tax bill. There is therefore a temptation to remove the property from assessment by ensuring that it becomes derelict, unable to command a rent, and therefore not liable for NNDR (Coalition for Economic Justice 2013).

The purpose of the reliefs and exemptions is presumably to subsidise particular types of business that are perceived to be of value to society. Some of the more significant of these exemptions and reliefs are described below (Exemptions and reliefs). Most were in place before the Local Government Finance Act (1988), but new ones have been introduced since then.

For most properties the Valuation Office Agency establishes the rateable value by fixing a rate per square metre, based on market evidence of the rents paid for similar uses in the local area, and applies this to the square meterage of the property in question. Since 1990, non-domestic property has been subject to a revaluation every five years to reflect sectoral and geographic shifts in the property market. The most recent revaluation was applied on 1 April 2010 (Valuation Office Agency 2010).

Mirrlees Review

In 2011 the Institute for Fiscal Studies published the Mirrlees Review. Its purpose was '*to identify what makes a good tax system for an open economy in the 21*st *century, and to suggest how the UK tax system could be reformed to move in this direction*' (James Mirrlees et al 2011). Mirrlees proposed a progressive, neutral tax system to '*raise the revenue that government needs to achieve its spending and distributional ambitions whilst minimising economic and administrative inefficiency, keeping the system as simple and transparent as possible, and avoiding arbitrary tax differentiation across people and forms of economic activity*' (James Mirrlees et al 2011: 471). His recommended reforms to the tax system as a whole are '*guided by economic theory, by the evidence on the impact of taxes, and by knowledge about the distribution of incomes and the workings of the economy*' (James Mirrlees et al 2011: 470).

One of his three recommendations for business taxes, and his principal conclusion in the category of taxation of land and property, is that in the case of non-domestic property '*There is a strong case for introducing a land value tax. In the foreseeable future, this is likely to mean focusing on finding ways to replace the economically damaging business rates system with a land value tax*' (James Mirrlees et al 2011: 404). But his advice comes with the important qualification '*if the practical difficulty of valuing land separately from the buildings on it can be overcome*' (James Mirrlees et al 2011: 477).

Stage 1

This section describes the proposed Stage 1 reform, which follows the recommendations for reform outlined by Mirrlees; contrasts some deficiencies of NNDR with the way that Stage 1 would address them; and concludes with an estimate of the levels of LVT that would be required in Stage 1 to achieve revenue-neutrality.

Proposed Stage 1 reform

The proposed Stage 1 reform is to replace NNDR with LVT that falls on ALL non-domestic property, in a revenue-neutral way.
This 'Stage 1 LVT' would be levied on the owner of each non-domestic property as a proportion of the annual market rent of the land, assessed on the assumption that the site is put to the highest and best use in accordance with the plans approved by the Local Planning Authority. All vacant and undeveloped land would be included within the definition of taxable non-domestic property. The valuation would be based on a computerised system of market data analysis and mass appraisal techniques, updated annually and based on market transactions.

Such a reform would immediately bring vacant and derelict land into the tax system and thereby spread the tax burden over a wider number of taxpayers. It would reduce the incentives to build up speculative holdings and land banks, as these would incur tax liabilities. Stage 1 would not remove Stamp Duty Land Tax, which would be removed in Stage 2.

Exemptions and reliefs

Some non-domestic properties are currently exempt from NNDR including farm land, farm buildings (but not those used for other business activities), fish farms, places of public religious worship, buildings used for training or welfare of disabled people and self-catering accommodation that is available to let for less than 140 days per year [GOV.UK 2013].

There are also rate relief schemes for a variety of properties including those that are in use by charities, not-for-profits, small businesses and rural businesses.

Governments have presumably chosen to subsidise these businesses and organisations by means of exemptions and reliefs from taxes rather than by direct subsidy payments because exemptions and reliefs are less visible, and government income that is forgone is less liable to be challenged than direct government expenditure. But any system of taxation should be neutral with respect to the type of business activity carried out on any site, or it will distort business use of land. Exemptions and reliefs distort the market, land use and the functioning of the economy. They also require the operation of the NNDR to police the boundaries between differently-taxed activities. This invites avoidance and evasion, increases administrative and compliance costs and creates incentives to use land in ways that are not optimal [James Mirrlees et al 2011: 472].

Any category of exemption or relief benefits the owner of the land not the tenant, whether it is applied to NNDR or to LVT. (If the owner is liable to pay the tax, exemption just reduces their tax liability. If the tenant is liable to pay the tax, the exemption or relief allows the owner to charge a higher rent than they could if the tenant were paying the full rate.) As a consequence exemptions and reliefs increase the value of land, and artificially increase the value of businesses that own their own land. The intention may be to benefit particular types of business, but that benefit is felt only by landlords and owner-occupiers – tenants lose as much from increased rents as they gain from reduced rates.

There may be a good a case for carrying over some exemptions and reliefs from NNDR to LVT for a limited period of time to reduce the impact of change, though no landowner should think of any exemption to LVT as a right. For agricultural land and charities the exemptions would continue in place for five years, following which a case would need to be made for their renewal (the law would contain a sunset clause (Glossary)).

Agricultural land

Agricultural land (and buildings) has been fully exempt from business rates since 1929. This benefits agricultural landlords and owner-occupiers, but not tenant farmers. It reduces the revenue available from business rates and, most importantly, it distorts land use by providing an incentive to purchase agricultural land as an investment. This inflates its price which raises the cost of entry to farming, increases the debts and interest payments of owner-occupier farmers and lowers their profitability.

Exemption of agricultural land from NNDR would be carried over and applied to LVT for 5 years after the start of Stage 1, and would then be subject to review (Issues to be considered in the feasibility study, below).

Charitable use

Reliefs and exemptions are available for sites that are used for public religious worship or charitable purposes. This distorts the land market by promoting charitable and faith use over commercial use, and should in principle not be retained beyond an initial five year period. Removal would penalise charities and faith bodies, and this would need to be mitigated by a direct subsidy from the state as discussed below (Issues to be considered in the feasibility study).

Small and rural businesses

Small businesses might lose from the withdrawal of exemption, though the market rent of their land, and so their LVT, is likely to be low – the reason for the current subsidy is that they are financially marginal. This low LVT would need to be protected by planning conditions that ensure that the land continues to be used for business, rather than residential, use. Labour-intensive businesses might gain from Stage 2 as their burden of employers' National Insurance Contributions would fall. If these factors were not enough to support these businesses they might require direct subsidies to replace the subsidy provided by rates relief, but for an interim period only.

Self-catering accommodation

Some self-catering accommodation is currently made available for less than 140 days per year in order to avoid the property becoming liable for NNDR. Ending this exemption would reduce the profitability of this approach and could be expected either to make more self-catering available throughout the year or to incentivise owners to use such properties for residential purposes, so increasing the amount of private rented housing available.

Problems caused by NNDR, and how Stage 1 will address them

This section describes the negative effects of NNDR on the use and development of land, on the economy as a whole, and on business profitability and competitiveness; and considers how their replacement by LVT addresses each of these.

Land use

Under-development and under-investment in land

There are several reasons why the current regime of NNDR causes under-development of land:

1. The damaging part of NNDR, which falls on buildings, discourages development. To make the optimal use of land it is necessary to invest the right amount in buildings and other improvements, neither too much nor too little, and this will differ from site to site. NNDR provides an incentive to make a sub-optimal investment simply to reduce the tax liability.

2. The part of NNDR that falls on land is not enough to discourage owners from keeping land idle in a land bank until it is needed (builders and supermarkets), or until it has risen in value (speculation).

3. Exemptions and reliefs from NNDR have unintended consequences – for example the absence of NNDR on derelict land makes it rational for its owners to keep, or even render, land derelict rather than to develop or sell it.

4. Reliefs for an empty period following a let to a charity have led to a proliferation of short-term lets (though this is not an essential feature of NNDR and could be resolved by repealing the Empty Property Rate legislation).

NNDR are levied using the same multiplier for buildings and for land, so investment in business premises leads to an increase in the NNDR. As Carmarthen's director of education has said about cases of severe disrepair:

> 'It's quite ironic that some of the schools are in such a poor state that the rateable value has come down. ..... It's so perverse as to be ridiculous. By improving the condition of the building — which is major priority (sic) — you bring upon yourself an increase in the rateable value. It just doesn't make sense' (Rob Sully 2011).

Replacement of NNDR by LVT provides an incentive to use and develop land, and so to efficient land use, compact developments, lower infrastructure costs and reduced urban sprawl:

1. It does not fall on buildings, and so does not inhibit investment in buildings and other improvements.

2. It falls on land and so provides a direct incentive either to develop relatively undeveloped land and to put it to good use or to sell it, leading to increased supply and lower land prices. This would reduce the borrowing needs, and indebtedness, of business

3. There are no exemptions or reliefs, and so no land is denied these benefits.

One of the sources of evidence that a Land Value Tax does indeed stimulate building and development is provided by cities in Pennsylvania that have adopted a 'split-rate' system in which the multiplier applied to the value of land is higher than the multiplier applied to the value of the improvements. Vacant sites are sold more readily, and more building permits are issued (Alanna Hartzog 1997). Every 1% shift in property taxes away from buildings and on to land is associated with a 16% increase in construction (Tony Vickers 2007: 51).

Threatening viable buildings

The Valuation Office Agency recognises that viable buildings have been vandalised, and even demolished, in order to render them exempt from NNDR (Valuation Office Agency 2013b). The 2008 extension of business rates to unoccupied but usable property may have exacerbated this vandalisation, which renders a property unusable and therefore exempt (Coalition for Economic Justice 2013).

Capturing planning gain

When agricultural land is given planning permission for residential use, its market value and market rent may rise a thousandfold. This private gain is the consequence of society making a planning decision. NNDR recoup part of this gain for society but they are only increased if the development actually takes place, and even then reflect only 41.3% of the increase in value of the property (usually less than 20% of the increase in land value).

Kate Barker (2004:78) identified four times since the Second World War that one-off taxes (betterment levies) on the development of land have failed to capture this increase in value that follows a favourable planning decision. These were the Development Charge under Clement Atlee in 1947, the Betterment Levy under Harold Wilson in 1967, Development Gains Tax under Ted Heath in 1973/4 and the Development Land Tax under Jim Callaghan in 1976. In each case the reason has been that landowners have been able to delay development until the legislation is repealed, because the legislation has never achieved cross-party support. More recent attempts to benefit from the grant of planning approval by imposing obligations on developers, such as Section 106 of the Planning and Compensation Act (1991) and the Community Infrastructure Levy (2010), capture only a small proportion of the gain and entail high uncertainties and transaction costs.

LVT is *not* a betterment levy, as its purpose is not to capture a one-off gain but an ongoing stream of rent. This market rent depends on a wide range of factors, one of which is a grant of planning permission. LVT ensures that the community, not the individual owner, benefits – and benefits from an ongoing stream of revenue not just the one-off benefit collected by a betterment levy.

Macroeconomics

One major macroeconomic benefit of replacing the NNDR with LVT is that it frees up land for production (Land use, above). Other benefits are that it removes the deadweight loss of taxation, stimulates the regeneration of areas where there is economic deprivation (Below), and has a counter-cyclical impact (Additional benefits of Stage 2, below).

Deadweight loss of taxation

Traditional taxes, including those falling on buildings, depress demand and so reduce both the amount of goods and services supplied and the price received by the producer (Figure 1) at the same time as increasing the price to the purchaser:

Reduced production

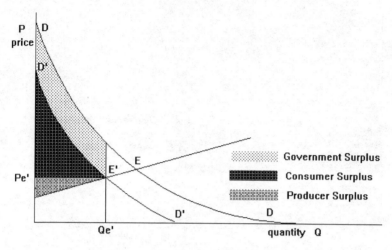

Figure 1 (based on Arnold Harberger 1964: 35)

This creates a lost surplus, or deadweight loss of taxation, which reduces economic activity and GDP (Figure 2):

Deadweight loss of taxation, or lost surplus

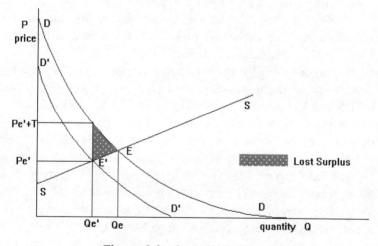

Figure 2 (based on Arnold Harberger 1964: 35)

Taxes on the value of land, the supply of which is inelastic, have a very different impact (Figure 3). As the supply curve is inelastic (vertical) there is no deadweight loss – the impact of the tax is simply to reduce the producer surplus, which in the case of land is its rent. In theory, taxes on the value of land are perfectly free from deadweight losses.

Optimal tax with no deadweight loss

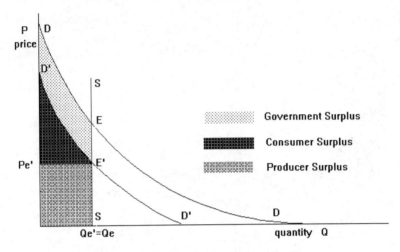

Figure 3 (based on Frank Ramsey 1927: 59)

Estimates of the magnitude of the deadweight loss of taxation vary widely, and are of limited applicability because they relate to taxes on income or are limited to the US economy. The classic estimate of the deadweight loss imposed by Income Tax was 2.5% of the revenue raised (Arnold Harberger 1964:51), based on the impact of the tax on the reduction in the number of hours worked. Subsequently it has been argued that this underestimates labour-supply elasticity because it ignores the way in which Income Tax causes employers to switch the compensation of workers to other improvements in the terms and conditions of work (e.g. working conditions and perks) and workers to change their patterns of consumption (e.g. by investing more in tax-deductible mortgage payments for housing). Martin Feldstein estimated that the total deadweight loss is around 30% of revenue raised, with a marginal rate of over 200% (Martin Feldstein 1999:680). A general equilibrium model of the US economy has been used to estimate the total deadweight loss or all taxes, compared with a non-distortionary lump-sum tax, at 13-24% of total tax revenue (Charles Ballard et al 1985:125).

Fred Harrison (2006a: 208) has established that the UK Treasury does not have any documentation on how the deadweight loss is calculated, and that it does not consider that it would be their role to carry out such a calculation. It does, however, use a figure of 30% for the Social Opportunity Cost of Exchequer Funds (SOCEF) for the purposes of cost benefit analysis (Department for Transport 2009), and this figure must reflect the deadweight loss of taxation.

The New Zealand Treasury suggests using an overall estimate of 20% for the Deadweight Loss (New Zealand Treasury 2005:18). Applying even this conservative estimate to the UK suggests that the replacement of NNDR by LVT in Stage 1 would reduce the deadweight loss of taxation by over £3bn per year [1], with the potential for even greater (revenue-neutral) economic stimulus in Stage 2. But whatever the numerical value of the deadweight loss of a tax on buildings and improvements, such as that imposed by NNDR, removing the deadweight loss increases economic growth.

Regeneration

Traditional forms of taxation cause some business sites to be unprofitable. If we imagine an economy without taxes, land in Figure 4 ranges from highly productive on the left to unproductive on the right. The land that is shaded dark is beyond the economic margin of production – it is not put to use because the return is not enough to pay the business costs including wages (the return to labour) and interest (the return to capital). 'Rent' refers to the return from the use of land, the annual market rent, and may be manifest either as a market rent paid by a tenant or as an imputed rent (Glossary) in the case of an owner-occupier.

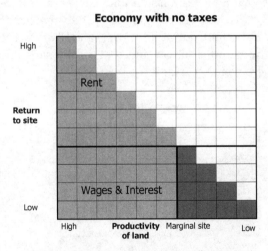

Figure 4 *(based on Tommas Graves 2011)*

Figure 5 shows the situation in which NNDR have been introduced, and all other variables such as planning conditions and GDP are assumed to be unchanged. Some sites that were previously used for

---

1 Assuming the UK revenue from NNDR is £27 billion (www.theguardian.com/news/datablog/2013/mar/20/budget-2013-tax-spending-visualised#zoomed-picture), and 60% of this is attributable to buildings (Coalition for Economic Justice 2013: 5).

production no longer generate enough return to pay the total cost of NNDR plus wages and interest. NNDR drives these sites out of use, and the margin moves to the left.

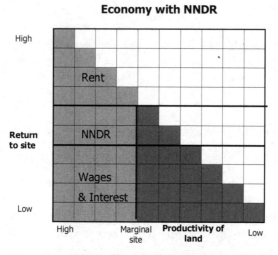

Figure 5 (based on Tommas Graves 2011)

Figure 6 shows LVT introduced in place of NNDR, and again all other variables such as planning permission and GDP are assumed to be unchanged. LVT falls less heavily on less productive land than on more productive land, and not at all on marginal land. The margin does not move and production continues at all the sites on which it occurred when there were no taxes.

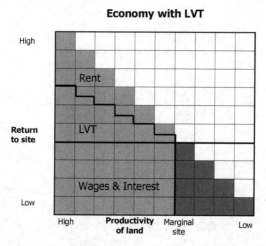

Figure 6 (based on Tommas Graves 2011)

Whereas conventional taxes reduce the amount of land that can support production, Land Value Tax does not. More land will be in productive use when subject to LVT than to NNDR, and this can be expected to support more people in employment. Also, as sites at the *economic* margin tend to cluster in areas of deprivation at the *geographical* margin, switching from NNDR to LVT provides an incentive for businesses to relocate from areas of high land value (for example South East England) to areas of lower land value. This stimulates the regeneration of deprived areas (Julian Pratt 2011: 53; Julie Froud et al 2011:47).

Business profitability and competitiveness

Profitability

If NNDR were to be replaced by LVT in a revenue-neutral way then sites that currently have the same total property value (land plus buildings), and so are paying the same level of NNDR, are likely after the reform to attract different levels of LVT. For example a large site consisting of bare ground in a city centre, with no buildings on it, may currently have the same total property value as an adjacent small site with a substantial building on it. The land makes up the whole of the value of the larger site, while it makes up only a proportion of the value of the smaller site.

Assuming there are similar planning conditions for the development of both sites, the owner of the developed site would pay less LVT than the owner of the undeveloped land, and less LVT than they used to pay in NNDR. The owner of the undeveloped site would pay more LVT than the owner of the developed site, and more LVT than they used to pay in NNDR. As a result, businesses that make efficient use of land will become even more profitable and competitive, while owners of under-developed land will acquire an incentive to develop or sell it. The financial position of tenants is unchanged.

Although there is a pressure to develop under-developed sites, the fear that land may generally become over-developed is unfounded. Under-developed land is released on to the market at affordable prices, protecting well-developed land, and if pressure does build up then any excess development should be contained by the planning system.

Landlords and tenants

Historically, business rates have been an occupier's tax and the liability to pay NNDR falls on tenants (for occupied properties). Establishing ownership can be problematic, particularly where the owner is not a UK resident, but rating law has nevertheless adapted so that it taxes owners directly where it is cheaper and easier to do so – for example in the case of caravan sites and houses adapted for occupation in parts.

The *incidence* (ultimate economic burden) of both NNDR and LVT falls on the owner not the tenant ^(Background, above). But the reform shifts the *liability* to pay the rates / tax from the tenant to the landlord. (The liability for businesses that own their premises, which can be thought of as both notional landlords and notional tenants, does not change as a result of the reform.)

This means that when LVT is introduced (on landlords) at the same time that NNDR are removed (from tenants), provided that other variables such as planning permission and GDP remain unchanged and that the switch is revenue-neutral:

- Where the NNDR and LVT are equal (a site that is developed to an average extent compared with similar sites), the introduction of LVT leaves the financial positions of both landlord and tenant unchanged. The tenant is free from NNDR but pays more rent, while the landlord receives more rent but has to pay the LVT.

- If the LVT is less than the NNDR (a well-developed site), when LVT is introduced tenants pay less tax but more rent and their financial position remains unchanged. The landlord receives more rent than they have to pay in tax, so they gain from the reform.

- If the LVT is greater than the NNDR (an under-developed site), when LVT is introduced the landlord will be able to pass on no more than an amount equal to the NNDR that has been removed – unless they are prepared to drive the tenant out of business. This is because the total of rent plus rates that the tenant can afford depends on the profitability of their business, which is unchanged in the short term by the introduction of LVT. The financial position of the tenant is unchanged (more rent but less tax), but the landlord faces a greater additional tax bill (for LVT) than the amount they receive in additional rent (equal to the old NNDR), and acquires an incentive to develop or sell their land [2].

---

2   When LVT is introduced on a rented property *without* other taxes being removed at the same time, however, the landlord *cannot* pass any of the additional tax on to the tenant unless the pre-existing rent was below the market level – again assuming that the landlord does not drive the tenant out of business by increasing the rent above the level warranted by the profitability of the tenant's business.

The international competitiveness of a business depends on many factors, one of which is the level of business taxation. Other things being equal, firms favour locating in low-tax environments. Although the headline rate of Corporation Tax is the most visible form of taxation, businesses are likely to be able to see beyond this to the total level of all business taxes – including NNDR or LVT.

The introduction of 'Stage 1 LVT' would reduce the property tax bill for businesses that make good use of their land, and so moving from NNDR to LVT would increase both their international competitiveness and the incentive for inward investment (Nicholas Boles 2011). At the same time it would discourage speculative inflows destined for investment in non-domestic land that would push up land prices and reduce the profitability of businesses.

Levels of LVT to be expected in Stage 1

NNDR is a combination of a Land Value Tax and a tax on buildings, each with a multiplier of 41.3%. Once the total market rent of all non-domestic properties has been assessed, a new multiplier will be calculated so that the overall change in Stage 1 is revenue-neutral. The new LVT multiplier for Stage 1 will approach 100% of the market rent of the land [3].

Stage 2

This section describes the proposed Stage 2 reform, discusses how the revenue from Stage 2 would be used to reduce and replace taxes that damage business, and sets out some additional benefits.

Proposed Stage 2 reform

A 'Stage 2 LVT' is introduced in addition to the 'Stage 1 LVT'. It is equal to 100% of any increase in the market rent of non-domestic land that occurs after the onset of Stage 2.

---

3   Land makes up between 30% and 60% of the total value of most industrial and commercial properties (Coalition for Economic Justice 2013: 5), with a plausible average of 40%. Assuming that the current annual value of the property is X, the annual value of the land is 40% of X. The current revenue for NNDR is 41.3% of X, so the whole of the annual value will have to be collected if it is to provide the same revenue as LVT.

Introduction of 'Stage 2 LVT'

Stage 2 begins after Stage 1 is complete *and* land values have risen above their value at the start of Stage 2. If at any time land values fall below this value, the Stage 1 arrangements prevail until land values exceed it.

Unlike 'Stage 1 LVT', where a multiplier is applied to the market rent of non-domestic land and calculated to ensure revenue-neutrality with respect to NNDR, 'Stage 2 LVT' applies a multiplier of *100%* to any increase in the market rent of land that has occurred since the start of Stage 2. 'Stage 2 LVT' will then rise and fall in line with land values and not, as with NNDR, be pegged to inflation (Retail Prices Index).

Phasing out other taxes on business

Any revenue stream that arises from the introduction of 'Stage 2 LVT' is retained by Treasury and used to reduce other taxes that damage business, in a way that is revenue-neutral vis à vis all taxes that damage business. These include VAT on refurbishment of buildings, Stamp Duty Land Tax, employers' National Insurance Contributions and eventually Corporation Tax. These would be replaced by LVT at a speed determined by the rate of growth, if any, in the market rent of land. These changes would contribute to tax simplification.

VAT on refurbishment of buildings

VAT is currently levied at 20% on the refurbishment of buildings and this discourages repair and refurbishment of existing buildings. This is exacerbated by exemption of the construction of new buildings from VAT. 'Stage 2 LVT' directly promotes the refurbishment of business properties.

Stamp Duty Land Tax

Stamp Duty Land Tax is a transaction tax that discourages mutually beneficial transactions, and has the consequence that properties may not be in the hands of those who can use them in the most efficient manner. This means that businesses may operate out of premises that are not the right size or location for them, which reduces their own profitability and that of other businesses that could make better use of their land (James Mirrlees et al 2011: 403). Mirrlees recommends removing Stamp Duty Land Tax as part of the revenue-neutral replacement of NNDR by LVT.

Removing Stamp Duty Land Tax would create a windfall gain in market value for existing property owners, as they would then be able to anticipate receiving the full value of their property at the time of sale without deduction of Stamp Duty Land Tax. If Stamp Duty Land Tax were to be removed as revenue becomes available from 'Stage 2 LVT', there would be no overall gains or losses to landowners as a whole. As in Stage 1, owners of well-developed properties would gain and owners of undeveloped properties would lose.

Stamp Duty Land Tax may currently be evaded by dividing a single transaction into several smaller transactions, or by fraudulently reducing the purchase price of a property that is declared to the Land Registry while the purchaser makes an undisclosed payment to the seller. Evasion of Stamp Duty Land Tax would disappear with the tax.

Employers' National Insurance Contributions

National Insurance Contributions are a tax on jobs and reduce the profitability of business. They fall most heavily on labour-intensive businesses, particularly those that employ the low-paid. As well as contributing to the deadweight loss of taxation they artificially favour capital-intensive over labour-intensive businesses and thus increase unemployment.

Reducing and ultimately removing employers' National Insurance Contributions would benefit businesses that are tenants and owner-occupiers, as their wage costs (including tax) would fall. This would be a pure gain for tenants, while owner-occupiers (who pay LVT) would benefit overall if they ran a labour-intensive business or made efficient use of their land but could lose if they had few workers. Landlords would not gain directly from removal of these contributions, and would be paying the LVT.

Additional benefits of Stage 2

Cap on non-domestic land values

'Stage 2 LVT' is equal to 100% of the increase in market rent that occurs after the start of Stage 2. The price at which an asset is bought and sold on the open market (its present value) is equal to the discounted value of future net cash flows from that asset, and the net cash flow from land will not increase over time after the start of Stage 2. 'Stage 2 LVT' would therefore immediately put an effective cap on the market value (sale price or capital value) of non-domestic land, and so prevent the cycles in non-domestic land value that have caused repeated banking failures and recessions around the world (Martin Wolf 2010).

23

Counter-cyclical impact

NNDR are designed to raise a steady stream of revenue, despite fluctuations in property values. They achieve this by adjusting the non-domestic rates multiplier each time there is a revaluation, to ensure that the total tax paid does not change across the business cycle. 'Stage 1 LVT' is calculated in the same way by adjusting the LVT multiplier at each revaluation.

During Stage 2 of the proposal, by contrast, the multiplier applied to any increase in the market rent of land after the start of Stage 2 is fixed at 100%. This would raise a new stream of revenue from all non-domestic land, but only if the economy was buoyant and the market rent of land had risen since the start of Stage 2. Revenue would fall during times when the market rent of land was falling. This would have an automatic counter-cyclical impact, reducing the tax burden in difficult times and increasing it when the economy was flourishing. This counter-cyclical macroeconomic benefit far outweighs the 'constant revenue' benefit of the current arrangements. It is dependent on frequent (at least annual) revaluations.

Self-funding infrastructure

Once 'Stage 2 LVT' is in place, new possibilities open up. The most dramatic arises from the impact on land values that a well-conceived infrastructure project, such as a new transport connection or broadband link, would have. The increase in market rents of properties that benefit from the infrastructure would be captured automatically as rising LVT and this stream of revenue could be used to fund the infrastructure investment, making it self-funding.

In April 2010 the Mayor of London introduced a Business Rate Supplement of 2p in the pound for all non-domestic properties with a rateable value of over £55,000, to fund a £4.1 billion contribution to Crossrail. The measure, which was well understood by the business community who will benefit from increases in both profitability and land values, was introduced with little controversy.

Compensation for adverse developments

There are many developments that may be necessary for society but which adversely affect nearby businesses including waste disposal sites, power plants and other sources of pollution. These developments lower the price of nearby land, and at present it is the owners of this land who bear the cost. Once Stage 2 is operational any fall in the market rent of land, which occurs for this or any other reason such as persistent traffic congestion or vandalism, would automatically reduce the LVT payable by the full amount of the annual loss. This would fully compensate non-domestic landlords who are adversely affected. It would be society – not the landlord – that bears the whole cost of these necessary developments, or deterioration that had been allowed to happen, by receiving a lower level of LVT.

Summary of anticipated benefits of the reform (Stages 1 & 2)

Macroeconomic benefit

- more than £3 billion per year stimulus to the economy in Stage 1, increasing in Stage 2

- in Stage 2 business taxes rise automatically in times of rapid economic growth, reducing the magnitude of any boom. They fall automatically in recessions [Page 15], providing a stimulus to business and the economy

- in Stage 2 a cap is effectively placed on the market value of non-domestic land, preventing boom and bust cycles in non-domestic land and the consequent risk to the banking system

Increased business profitability and international competitiveness

- property taxes are reduced for businesses that make efficient use of their land

- property taxes are reduced for businesses operating on marginal land

- the business property tax base is broadened

- businesses benefit from increased infrastructure investment

- in Stage 1 there is a one-off loss in market value for owners of land but a windfall gain for owners of buildings and other improvements. In consequence owners of well-developed land will be rewarded by reduced levels of taxation and increased property values. Owners of poorly-developed land will be encouraged to develop the property to its highest and best use, or to sell it to somebody who will do so

- in Stage 2 a cap is effectively placed on the market value of non-domestic land, reducing the capital costs for future start-up businesses

- in Stage 2 VAT on the refurbishment of buildings, Stamp Duty Land Tax and employers' National Insurance Contributions are reduced, and eventually removed

Regeneration of under-developed areas

- reduced business taxation in (geographically marginal) areas that are currently unattractive will encourage new businesses to locate there, and existing businesses to expand locally

Self-funding infrastructure

- well-conceived infrastructure (e.g. transport, fast broadband) increases the profitability of the businesses that are positively affected, and so the value of their land. This results in higher levels of LVT, which may in turn be used to finance the infrastructure and allow it to become self-funding

- owners are automatically compensated if their environment deteriorates (by the amount that their rent falls)

Reduced tax avoidance and evasion

- reduced vandalisation of potentially viable buildings to avoid NNDR

- reduced evasion of VAT, Stamp Duty Land Tax and National Insurance Contributions in Phase 2

Optimal land use

- reduced incentives to hold land for speculation and land banking

- financial incentives that bring all land into optimal use, increase the supply of land and lower land prices

- no tax penalties for developing or improving buildings

- incentive to ensure that all non-domestic land is in the hands of those who can make best use of it

- efficient use of all land leads to compact development, reduction in urban sprawl with reduced infrastructure costs, less pressure on the green belt and reduction in carbon dioxide emissions.

Issues to be considered in the feasibility study

The reforms proposed by Mirrlees and explored further in this paper require careful design, and would first require a feasibility study carried out by Treasury. This section sets out some of the issues to be considered in this feasibility study. The range of stakeholders that would be affected and the need for cross-party consensus mean that the feasibility study should explore its widest implications.

Impact on business

Agriculture

Tenants are not directly affected by the reform, but as other taxes on business are phased out in Stage 2 they would gain – particularly from the reduction in employers' National Insurance Contributions, which would incentivise more labour-intensive agriculture.

Agricultural landowners (whether landlord or owner-occupier) would be protected during transition to Phase 1 by an initial five-year exemption that would then be reviewed and possibly extended (Stage 1 Exemptions and reliefs, above), bearing in mind that the cost of this exemption is borne by non-agricultural businesses. Once this exemption came to an end, agricultural landowners would face a new tax, and a loss in the market value of their properties.

The yield of agricultural land is at present several times less than it is for other types of non-domestic property, indicating that the price of this land has a speculative element as an investment. For example, a member of the Henry George Society of Devon is a hill farmer. In 2007 he acquired an agricultural tenancy on part of his farm at the market rate of £50 per acre per year, which (assuming a yield of 5%) would imply a market value (purchase price) of around £1000 per acre. In the same year he paid £6,000 per acre to purchase the adjacent land, of the same quality, on the open market.

Inflation of the price of agricultural land, caused by subsidies as well as the exemption from NNDR, does serious damage to farming:

- it discourages farmers from selling land that they are not using to full efficiency

- it encourages farmers' natural propensity to buy land that is some distance from their farm, even when they know that they cannot farm it as efficiently as their home farm

- it encourages investors and wealthy hobbyists to acquire land from active farmers

- it increases the entry costs for young people who want to enter farming

- mortgage repayments, on borrowings that reflect the investment rather than the business value of the land, make it extremely difficult for owner-occupier farms to operate profitably.

Introducing LVT would reduce (and in Stage 2 remove) the speculative element to current agricultural land values. This would benefit the agricultural sector as a whole, both by reducing the levels of debt of farming owner-occupiers and by making it easier for new entrants to agriculture. Agriculture would also benefit from a long-term change in incentives to favour more labour-intensive rather than capital-intensive farming methods.

In spite of the benefits of the reform to agriculture as a whole, agricultural landowners would be the group to experience the greatest loss, in both rents and capital value, as a result of the reform. The losses by landowners are not due to LVT itself but to the removal of the long-term subsidy to agricultural landowning provided by exemption from NNDR, and to the expectations to which this has given rise. It is not difficult to imagine that a strong case would be made for renewals of the five year exemption.

The feasibility study would need to explore both the benefits to the economy as a whole and the costs to agricultural landowners of the removal of the exemption from 'Stage 1 LVT', in order to inform the debate about how long to continue it.

Whatever the outcome of these negotiations about renewal of Stage 1 exemptions, it is essential that Stage 2, and 'Stage 2 LVT', should be introduced on agricultural land at the same time as on all other non-domestic land. Stage 2 captures only the increase in value that occurs after the start of Stage 2, and while having no impact on current levels of rent and capital value it does put a cap on their future values. There should be no question of exemption from Stage 2.

Non-domestic landowners

During the revenue-neutral Stage 1, owners of well-developed non-domestic property will experience a windfall gain in its net market rent and its market value. This will increase both their revenue and their capital assets, and reduce their indebtedness. Owners of un-developed non-domestic property will experience a one-off loss in net market rent and in market value, and this will provide an incentive either to develop or to sell their land.

The feasibility study would need to consider the extent of this burden on owners of un-developed non-domestic property, and whether any mitigating measures should be put in place. The most extreme option that might need to be considered, even though it would delay for a decade or two the full benefits of the reform, would be not to implement Stage 1 at all but to move immediately to the implementation of Stage 2.

Investors in non-domestic property

The private investment market is highly concentrated in high value properties, which are most likely to benefit from the replacement of NNDR by LVT. Owner-occupiers tend to own the less valuable properties, and are most likely to experience a loss in the market value of their property as a result of the change (Coalition for Economic Justice 2013: 2).

During Stage 2, if the economy is buoyant then market rents will tend to rise and LVT will rise along with them. Non-domestic landowners will not suffer any erosion in the market value of their investments from this increase in LVT, but they can no longer anticipate that the market value of their property will rise over the course of time. This means that if their business model depends on these capital gains, their business is likely to be unprofitable. This is, however, unlikely to affect many businesses as all landowners retain the full value that their whole property has at the start of Stage 2, and the rational expectation is that this price will have built in the expected gains in market rent that had been anticipated before the introduction of LVT.

Banks and other institutional investors have a long history of investing in non-domestic property at inflated prices during property booms, and suffering bankruptcy or government bail-out when the bust comes. Stage 2, once in place, will protect them (and the taxpayer) from such losses in the future.

The feasibility study should explore the risks and benefits to investors and their lenders as well as to landowners.

Charities and places of public worship

LVT would impose a new burden of tax on charities and places of public worship, and this would be undesirable. The apparent solution of continuing to exempt such land from property taxation contravenes the principle that all non-domestic land should be subject to the same tax regime.

Transferring the ownership of properties into the name of a charity has become a significant device for tax avoidance in the USA, and questions are currently being asked about similar issues in the UK (Radio 4 Today programme 9/7/13).

One possible mitigating factor for the charity or faith group is the planning system, which could ensure that any burden of LVT on charities would be small by imposing a planning condition that a site must be used for the purpose of charitable activity or public worship. In this situation the market rent would be set by competition amongst charities and faith organisations but not other businesses, and would therefore be lower than it would be in a completely open market.

If the planning conditions for a site include enforceable provisions for free public access, preservation of landscape, environmental sustainability and prohibition of new building then there would be few people or organisations that would want to purchase it, and its value would be low. Indeed if the planning conditions were sufficiently onerous then there might be no potential purchasers. In this situation an LVT regime could take the land into collective (state) ownership or it could, if it wished, ensure the ongoing management of such land as private property by inviting bids for a subsidy (negative rent).

In spite of these planning measures, some charities and faith groups might find that they had a higher burden of LVT than they had of NNDR. The remedy for this is not to exempt charities from LVT but to provide an alternative form of government subsidy to charities.

The feasibility study should explore what alternative form of government subsidy would be appropriate for charities and faith groups.

Non-domestic leases

Non-domestic leases generally stipulate that any increase in rates is to be paid by the tenant. The feasibility study should explore how Stage 2 LVT can be introduced, payable by the landlord, without LVT being interpreted as 'rates' and triggering these clauses.

Valuation for Land Value Tax

The major practical challenge for this reform is to establish an agreed way to value land separately from the buildings on it. In the UK, small scale exercises to estimate the value of land alone have taken place twice in Whitstable [Hector Wilks 1964 & 1974] and once in Oxford [Land Value Tax working party 2005], and in each of these cases the valuers have reported that there are no significant problems in arriving at the valuation of land alone. This has also been the case in Australia, the USA, Canada and Denmark where LVT or split-rate taxes have been applied [Robert Andelson 2000].

Valuation of land (separate from improvements) is not common practice in the UK and there is a severe shortage of UK-based valuers with the necessary skills and experience (though valuations of replacement costs are routinely carried out for insurers and developers). There are particular challenges associated with the complex nature of non-domestic land tenure in the UK, but there are ways of tackling these. It will be essential to include in the discussions those with experience of jurisdictions where LVT is in place, and UK experts such as the Professional Land Reform Group (www.landvaluescape.org), as well as the Valuation Office Agency, the Royal Institution of Chartered Surveyors (www.rics.org) and the Institute of Revenues, Rating and Valuation (www.irrv.net).

Valuation of land – possible methods and their drawbacks

Methods of valuation that are appropriate for NNDR may also be fit for purpose for LVT, provided that only a small proportion of the market rent of land is being collected as LVT. However when up to 100% of the market rent of land is captured as LVT, as with both 'Stage 1 LVT' and 'Stage 2 LVT', a different approach is needed (Valuation for LVT – practice, below).

Market rent and market value

The valuation on which LVT is based is the annual market rent of land, not the market value (sale price or capital value). Market rent and market value are related by the 'yield' – the market rent divided by the market value.

The 'gold standard' for valuing a site is to expose it to the open market and to discover the price that it achieves. A market for sale reveals its market value, a market for rent reveals its market rent. If most market transactions are for sale not for rent, it may be necessary to establish the market *value* of a site and multiply this by the yield. The courts have accepted for NNDR that although the short-term yield varies (e.g. with the short-term interest rate), a valuer may use the long-term rate of return that a landlord can expect from this class of property (Roger Emeny & Hector Wilks 1984:172). But using the market value is complicated by the fact that yield varies amongst different classes of property and in different locations, and would change with the introduction of LVT.

Valuation by comparison

Where a property has not recently been exposed to the market, the main alternative to exposing it to the market once again is to make a valuation by identifying other 'comparables' – sites, similar to the index

31

site (Glossary) in location and other characteristics, that have themselves been recently exposed to the market. Since these 'comparables' are in reality 'near-comparables', and have been exposed to the market at different times, valuation by comparison requires judgement by a professional valuer.

This approach is greatly assisted by the use of Geographic Information Systems, which make it possible to display valuation information visually from a database of land values (e.g. AREIS 2013) as a 'landvaluescape' (Tony Vickers 2009). It is possible to identify factors that influence land value by means of multiple regression analysis, and to value multiple properties from a knowledge of these factors – Computer Assisted Mass Appraisal.

Any approach that uses direct valuation by comparison to arrive at the value of land (without buildings) must use, as comparables, other sites without buildings. In a developed economy comparable empty sites may be difficult to find. Where this is the case, an alternative is to use comparables that are encumbered with buildings, and to make an allowance for the value of these buildings. The best estimate of this value is the Depreciated Replacement Cost (Glossary), an estimate also used by the residual method.

Residual method

The residual method (also known as the Contractor's Test) adds the estimated Depreciated Replacement Cost of the building to the market value of the land to arrive at a market value of the whole property (Frances Plimmer 1998 6.6.12). The Lands Tribunal has several times referred to it as a 'method of last resort' (Roger Emeny & Hector Wilks 1988: 173), principally as it appears to be based on the assumption that the current value of a building is equal to the price of its construction. Value and price are not the same, as the building may be physically obsolescent (due to deterioration) and/or functionally obsolescent (either because it has been constructed to too high a specification for the site when it was built, or because it not longer has the same functional use that it had at that time). In order to take account of this, a valuer must assess the value of a functionally equivalent 'simple substituted building' built using contemporary materials, and also take account of physical deterioration. In spite of their criticisms, the Lands Tribunal have also ruled that the in the hands of an experienced valuer this can be as precise as any other method (Roger Emeny & Hector Wilks 1988: 173).

Land as a proportion of the whole property

Another approach may be used when the value of the whole property is known. The value of land as a proportion of the value of the whole property is first estimated for comparable properties. The value of the whole index site is then multiplied by this proportion to arrive at the value of the land element of the index site.

Alternative approaches to valuation of property (land plus buildings)

Evidence of comparables is not available for all types of land use. A range of alternative methods have been used including the profits ('income and expenditure' or 'accounts') approach, which estimates the (potential) trading surplus of the business and so the rent that it could be expected to pay (Roger Emeny & Hector Wilks 1984). And because of the limitations of the alternatives, some providers of utilities are valued for NNDR using a statutory formula.

Valuation for LVT – practice

In Stage 1 the valuation is carried out by an assessor. In Stage 2 it is carried out in and by the market, and kept up to date by an assessor using Computer Assisted Mass Appraisal.

In Stage 1 the task is to take the current market value of the land plus improvements on each plot (already established for NNDR) and apportion this between the land and the buildings. This will be contentious, but assessors will be able to draw both on knowledge of the land value of comparable vacant sites and measures of the Depreciated Replacement Cost of the building on the index site. All of these methods are tried and tested, and this valuation needs to be carried out once only.

In Stage 2 a New Land Market will establish, whenever a property is sold or leased, both the market rent of the land *and* the Land Value Tax.

The role of the assessor will be to update land valuations by comparison with recently marketed comparables, and to establish the Depreciated Replacement Cost of new buildings only.

New Land Market

Valuation for LVT faces some challenges that are similar to those faced by NNDR, such as:

- there may be no, or few, suitable comparables
- 'comparables' are at best only near-comparables

- market valuations are obtained at different times and have to be adjusted for the date of valuation
- sufficient market data about the value of leases, rather than sales, may not be available.

But there are additional challenges that are specific to LVT:

- the valuation needs to reflect the highest and best use, not the current use
- most comparisons are with sites encumbered with buildings
- the market *value* of land is zero where LVT is levied at 100% of market rent, and effectively capped when it is levied at 100% of the increase in market rent. This means that market values cannot be used to calculate market rents or levels of LVT even if the yield is known. Valuations have to be based on market transactions for annual values (rents).

None of the methods described above (Valuation of land - possible methods and their drawbacks) are, therefore, fit for purpose without modification when LVT is levied at close to 100% of the market rent. The value of land will need to be established in a market for rent, not a market for sale. And all property transactions, not just those involving bare undeveloped sites, will need to be taken into consideration.

To meet these challenges, a New Land Market has been proposed (Julian Pratt 2011: 116). Here, property transfers are made at auctions in which the bids are for annual payments of the LVT, equal to the (gross) market rent. The principle is the same as that for the spectrum auctions, or indeed for rail franchises. The New Land Market requires the bidder to undertake to pay the full Depreciated Replacement Cost of the buildings to the seller if the bid is successful. It allows market transactions on developed sites to establish directly the market rent of the land alone.

In the New Land Market the Depreciated Replacement Cost is *not* subtracted from an estimate of the market value of the whole property, but is made available to the bidder *before* they decide their bid that may determine the market rent and LVT. The Depreciated Replacement Cost takes full account of any obsolescence, and so of any difference between price (of construction) and value. So the New Land Market is not the same as the residual method – though both make use of the Depreciated Replacement Cost and face the same challenges when assessing the degree of depreciation.

34

It is a well-accepted principle of property taxation that the value should be based on the form of tenure prevailing in the market. Adopting the New Land Market creates a new form of tenure – 'stewardship' (Julian Pratt 2011: 4) – and all valuations are based on this form of tenure.

The aim of Land Value Taxation is to ensure that everybody benefits from the wealth of the natural world while proprietors own, in the conventional sense, artefacts like buildings. The New Land Market recognises that land has artefacts attached to it (buildings and other improvements), and allots to the owner a fair price for these.

The feasibility study should consider the practicality and cost of the New Land Market.

Multiple owners of property on a single site

It is not uncommon for there to be multiple owners of properties on a single plot of land.

Where there are comparable vacant sites, one approach that can be used is to establish the market rent of the whole site and then to allocate the market rent of the whole site amongst the owners (for example in proportion to the market value of the improvements).

Where there are not enough vacant sites to provide comparables, an alternative approach is first to establish the market value of the improvements belonging to each owner and then to use these values in the New Land Market to establish the market rent of each property. The market rent of the whole site can then be defined to be equal to the sum of the market rents of the individual properties – though this would have to be specified in the legislation.

The feasibility study should consider these alternatives and recommend which to adopt. This should include consideration of how to apportion any 'marriage value' (Glossary).

Long leaseholds

If a property is held on a lease that allows for revisions of the rent that are sufficiently frequent to ensure that the rent is close to market levels, the landowner is the beneficiary of the whole of the market rent and should be liable to pay the LVT. If on the other hand the rent is held constant over a long period of time, as is the case with some domestic leasehold properties, the leaseholder may receive more of the (imputed) market rent of the site than the landlord and have a financial interest in the property. In this case the market rent of the leasehold interest in the site would need to be assessed and collected from the leaseholder. The

35

feasibility study should consider possible ways to assess the liability of the long leaseholder, if indeed this is a significant issue for non-domestic property.

Hosting the valuations

The Valuation Office Agency provides the government with the valuations and property advice required to support taxation. They produce the rating lists that contain the rateable values on which local billing authorities levy the NNDR, and are the natural choice to host the valuations. The feasibility study should explore what resources the Agency would require for this purpose.

Appeals

Ratepayers can at present make an appeal against the rateable value assigned to their property by proposing an amendment to the rating list. The process is complex, with a first stage dealt with by a Valuation Tribunal and the possibility of further appeal to the Lands Tribunal.

As the 'gold standard' for any valuation is the price actually achieved in the market, once LVT has been introduced any proprietor must be allowed and enabled, at any time, to appeal against this valuation by offering the property on the open market and bidding what they believe to be its market rent. The feasibility study should consider the necessary safeguards.

Keeping valuations up to date and on public display

If a property tax is to be equitable, it must be based on up-to-date valuations. But some win and some lose from each revaluation, and revaluations are politically easier to avoid than to carry out. The NNDR are based on quinquennial valuations. Because revaluations that are so infrequent may result in a large increase in the burden of rates for some properties, a self-funding system of transition reliefs has been provided to smooth the transition.

Information is, however, nowadays available on a real-time basis from property transaction data. LVT would be based on revaluations that take place at least annually, using technology that is already available. The feasibility study should explore how to put this in place.

The market rent assessed for each site should be held in a publicly accessible database and displayed as maps of the 'landvaluescape' (Tony Vickers 2009). Systems such as these (AREIS 2013) have the advantage that public scrutiny and feedback can lead to improved data quality as well as providing complete transparency. The feasibility study should examine how best to make the information available at the least cost, and how to receive feedback from the public. This includes exploration of ways to tackle any legal blocks to making this information publicly available.

Implications for planning

These reforms would put the planning system at the heart of business taxation, as the market rent of land is absolutely dependent on the planning conditions placed upon it.

Some necessary changes that can be anticipated are:

- each Local Planning Authority will have to provide an up-to-date, detailed and definitive Local Area Plan for all land in their area, following widespread public consultation and before the implementation of LVT. Permitted use(s) would be specified for each site and there could be no changes until a complete replacement plan was adopted after an appropriate interval

- the planning system would find itself subject to greater public scrutiny and would need to make its decisions more transparent and democratic

- LVT reflects the highest and best use of the land based on the Local Area Plan, and the increased LVT resulting from a grant of planning permission would provide an immediate financial stimulus to carry out the work as soon as possible. Planning decisions become prescriptive rather than permissive

- owners might seek to have planning conditions *imposed* on their land in order to keep LVT bills down, rather than seeking to have planning conditions *removed* to increase the market value of their property

- owners might seek permission to use their property for domestic purposes in order to avoid a LVT that is imposed only on non-domestic properties

- Local Planning Authorities would need more financial resources, particularly to ensure democratic transparency and to contest appeals from developers who have deep pockets to fund their legal advisors.

The feasibility study should explore how the planning system should identify the challenges, how it would need to respond, and what extra resources it would require. In particular it should explore whether, and under what circumstances, the permitted uses of a site set out in the

Local Area Plan could be challenged and changed.

Restrictive covenants

An owner might seek to impose a restrictive covenant on their property because this, like planning conditions, would reduce their liability for LVT. When society chooses to impose restrictions on land use (through the planning mechanism), it is right for society to bear the cost (through reduced public revenue from LVT). But privately imposed restrictive covenants could provide a mechanism for tax avoidance. They are not permitted to influence the current assessment of rateable value (Frances Plimmer 1998 5.5.5), and the feasibility study should explore how to prevent them from affecting the valuation for LVT.

Retaining new domestic developments within the LVT regime

Once Stage 1 is in place, owners of un-developed land will be paying LVT. If a site is *then* developed for housing the completed homes could be expected to retain their non-domestic classification and pay LVT or they could, on the grounds that they are now domestic properties, be expected to pay Council Tax. There is a choice.

If properties were retained in the LVT regime there would be a number of consequences:

1. The homeowner in the LVT regime would pay more in LVT than their neighbour, living in an identical home built before the introduction of LVT, would be paying in Council Tax [4].

---

4   Council Tax - a 'back of the envelope' example:
- A property is allocated to Band A if its value on 1st April 1991 was less then £40,000
- A property is allocated to Band H if its value on 1st April 1991 was more than £320,000

Using the calculator at moneysavingexpert.com, which uses Nationwide house price data, the current (2013 Q1) values of properties in these bands are very approximately:
- Band A – less than £ 120,000 – implying an annual market rent of less than £6,000
- Band H – more than £ 980,000 – implying an annual market rent of more than £49,000

The current annual Council Tax charges (including amounts collected for county council, district council, parish council, fire & rescue and police & crime commissioner) are (for South Hams in Devon):
- Band A - £1,018 p/a, (more than 17% of market rent of whole property)
- Band H - £3,053 p/a, (less than 6% of market rent of whole property)

(continued)

2. Land (and so properties) subject to LVT would have a lower market value than land (and so properties) subject to Council Tax.

3. A homeowner paying LVT would therefore be able to purchase a home at a more affordable price than if they were paying Council Tax. This would require a lower deposit and result in lower mortgage payments.

4. As the market rent of land (net of LVT) in the LVT regime does not rise over time, the owner would have an asset that does not increase (or decrease) in value in the way that it would if it was subject to Council Tax. This arrangement would insulate the owner from fluctuations in the housing market and, in general, make home ownership less desirable as a financial investment (though also less liable to result in negative equity). This could reduce demand, lower both its market rent and its LVT, and make such housing even more affordable.

5. Overall, the owner of a home in the LVT regime would have a radically different experience compared with the owner of a home paying Council Tax. The upside in the LVT regime is that their home would be substantially more affordable to purchase, they would have lower levels of mortgage debt and mortgage payments, and there would be no risk of negative equity. The upside for taxpayers generally is that this would generate more revenue than Council Tax. In order to maintain revenue-neutrality, this revenue should be used to reduce other taxes on domestic properties – starting with VAT on the refurbishment of domestic buildings and moving on to Stamp Duty Land Tax.

Suppose that the value of the land is equal to 50% of the value of the whole property
- Band A LVT would be less than £3,000, compared with NNDR of £1,018
- Band H LVT would be more than £24,500, compared with NNDR of £3,053

If the value of the land were equal to 20% of the value of the whole property
- Band A LVT would be less than £1,200, compared with NNDR of £1,018
- Band H LVT would be more than £9,800, compared with NNDR of £3,053

So the claim that the LVT is higher than the Council Tax holds for low-value properties even if and makes up only 20% of the value of the whole property, and for high-value properties even if land makes up only 6% of the whole property.

NB this calculation relates ONLY to domestic properties that are built after the replacement of NNDR by LVT, on land classified as non-domestic at the time that LVT is introduced. It is NOT a proposal to introduce LVT on land that is currently classified as domestic.

6. The downside for the owner in the LVT regime is that they would pay more in LVT than their neighbour pays in Council Tax, and they would not benefit from the rising house prices that characterise the upswing of the economic cycle. The downside for banks and other mortgage lenders is that their income from mortgage interest would fall as the value of mortgages fell.

The feasibility study would need to explore these impacts in more detail, and the implications of subjecting such properties to Council Tax or to LVT.

Including in the LVT regime residential properties that are owned by companies

The Annual Tax on Enveloped Buildings (previously Annual Residential Property Tax) is a tax that is currently levied on dwellings worth more than £2 million that are owned by corporate entities. The feasibility study should explore whether all corporately owned property, including dwellings, should be included in the LVT regime in Stage 2. This would allow the Annual Tax on Enveloped Buildings to be removed, contributing to tax simplification.

Establishing ownership and enforcing payment

The collection of NNDR is enforced by the billing authority, which has to take the matter of non-payment to the magistrates' court. LVT is levied on the owner not, as it is for the NNDR, on the occupier so it is important to be able to establish who the owner of any property is. This may be difficult, particularly where it is unoccupied and the owner is not UK-based.

The feasibility study should set out the steps needed to ensure the compulsory registration of all non-domestic land, which would not require primary legislation. It should also explore how to ensure that LVT is paid on time, for example by:

- permitting, where necessary, the collection of LVT from a tenant and requiring them to deduct it from the rent they pay
- making freehold property rights conditional on the regular payment of LVT (which would also provide landowners with an incentive to ensure that all land is included in the register)
- setting unpaid LVT (with interest on the unpaid sum) as a charge against the value of the property at the Land Registry so that it can, at worst, be recouped at the time of sale or transfer.

Transitional arrangements

After the necessary preparations, Stage 1 should be phased in over a period of time, perhaps two to five years. During this time owners of non-domestic properties would pay a decreasing proportion of NNDR and an increasing proportion of LVT. The feasibility study should consider the timetable that is appropriate.

Some of the impacts on business of the proposed reform are predictable, but there will inevitably be unexpected consequences. The feasibility study should bring together a range of stakeholders to explore these possible consequences and, if necessary, how to mitigate them during transition. The stakeholders should include business people from a range of sectors, sizes and types of property holding (tenant, landowner, owner-occupier, investor, lender), local authorities (as both landowners and planners), government agencies, the Valuation Office Agency, Land Registry, charities and community groups.

Pilot areas

Both Stage 1 and Stage 2 reforms should be piloted before they are applied to the whole country, in order to identify and remedy any unexpected negative consequences. Ideally the pilot areas would be chosen by inviting local authorities to express an interest, and selected to include areas in greatest need of regeneration. These reforms could form the basis of a new sort of Enterprise Zone.

The feasibility study should explore how best to implement the removal of VAT on refurbishment of buildings, Stamp Duty Land Tax and employers' National Insurance Contributions in Stage 2 in this context; it should also consider whether the revenue-neutrality of the pilots should be at national or local level.

The feasibility study should also establish how the pilots would be evaluated – in particular the costs of the reform (including the costs of valuation, re-valuation, maintaining a public register, appeals and cost to the planning system) and its benefits (including the reduction in vacant and derelict land, increased new building and refurbishment, increased employment and economic activity and the reduction of other taxes).

Legal considerations

There are likely to be legal challenges to this proposal to introduce LVT. This might be on the human rights grounds that it represents a confiscation of property or an invasion of privacy. Or it could be on the

41

grounds that it contravenes the Official Secrets Act (which applies to some information about land ownership). The feasibility study would need to consider these issues, and how the reform could be drafted to avoid successful challenge.

Costs

The feasibility study should estimate the costs of each element of the proposal.

Current academic and political support

There was significant political support for LVT in the first half of the 20th century, which led to several attempts to introduce legislation in the UK (Lloyd George in 1909, Philip Snowden in 1931 and Herbert Morrison in 1939). Economists have long understood that the most efficient taxes fall on factors whose supply is inelastic [Frank Ramsey 1927], but LVT was academically as well as politically marginalised throughout the latter half of the 20th century. There has, however, been a sea-change amongst economists over the last decade, triggered in part by the ease with which other forms of taxation can be shifted to low-tax jurisdictions or avoided in other ways [Economist 2013].

In the UK the report by Sir James Mirrlees (advocating the replacement of NNDR by LVT as part of a wider reform of the tax benefit system) aligns a Nobel Prizewinner in optimal taxation with this reform [James Mirrlees et al 2011: 377]. Internationally the OECD has ranked taxes on immovable property as the least distorting tax instrument in terms of reducing long-run GDP per capita [OECD 2010:10], and a recent IMF working paper recognised the particular efficiency advantages of taxes on immovable property – particularly a tax on land value, which maximises the incentives to put land to its optimal use [John Norregaard 2013:16]. Even the *Economist*, which not so long ago characterised supporters of LVT as cranks who are not above handing out leaflets on street corners [Economist 1998: 96], has endorsed this IMF paper [Economist 2013].

The case for LVT has been made, in this paper as in the Mirrlees Review, on efficiency grounds. But there are also powerful ethical arguments for raising fees or charges for the use of the natural world – including land [Julian Pratt 2011: 97]. These include the claim that title to land can only be justified by the payment of a fee as compensation for excluding others from the land, and the claim that the value of a plot of land is created not by its owner but by the society that exists around the plot and provides the infrastructure, social stability and business opportunities that give it 'location value'. These ethical claims find resonance with the general public when they are set out clearly, and there is growing support for such a reform amongst political commentators and bloggers (e.g. Mark Braund 2010, Larry Elliott 2010, Philip LeGrain 2010, Polly Toynbee 2009, Mark Wadsworth 2013,), amongst informal networks (George Monbiot 2013), and in political parties.

The Green Party, for whom LVT has always been central, made a firm manifesto commitment for the 2010 election and Caroline Lucas MP introduced a private members bill to advance LVT in 2013.

The Co-operative Party (which has 26 sitting MPs and is affiliated to, and runs candidates with, the Labour party) also made a manifesto commitment to LVT in 2010.

Support for LVT has traditionally been strong amongst Liberals, and the proposal to replace NNDR by LVT was written in to the Liberal Democrats' 2010 election manifesto. Its *Fairer Tax* policy paper, adopted in September 2013, commits the party to a full scale review of *how* LVT might best be implemented 'early in the next parliament' if they find themselves in government again.

The first Labour manifesto of 1909 included proposals for the introduction of LVT, and the Labour Land Campaign supports LVT, but it is not party policy. The TUC has passed a motion supporting an economic strategy that explores the benefits of Land Value Taxes (Trades Union Congress 2011); and there is active support from the Public and Commercial Services Union (PCS) and the National Union of Rail, Maritime and Transport Workers (RMT) (Dave Wetzel 2013). In the last Labour leadership contest two candidates, John McDonnell MP (John McDonnell 2007) and Andy Burnham MP (Andy Burnham 2010) publicly supported LVT.

Opposition to LVT by the Conservative party is in part a response to proposals that have been made to apply LVT to domestic properties, though Conservatives share with many others a concern about the practical challenges of valuation. Occasional voices in the Conservative party recognise the potential benefits of LVT for business profitability and competitiveness – Nick Boles, MP for Grantham and the coalition's parliamentary under-secretary for planning, wrote in the Financial Times to support its introduction on non-domestic land (Nicholas Boles 2011).

The implementation of LVT would need significant cross-party support to survive the electoral cycle. The key obstacle is that most members of the public (seven out of eight) have never heard of it and do not think that it is fair. By contrast, the majority of those who are already at all 'in the know' believe that it is fair (Coalition for Economic Justice 2012). The results of this poll (even though it focused on domestic rather than non-domestic land) suggest that it could be possible to build widespread public support for the proposal set out in this paper.

Conclusion

The current regime of National Non-Domestic (Business) Rates (NNDR) encourages the under-use and under-development of non-domestic land and penalises businesses that invest in buildings and other improvements, reducing their profitability and competitiveness. Replacing NNDR with Land Value Taxation (LVT) would provide more than £3 billion a year in economic stimulus as the deadweight loss of taxation of non-domestic premises was withdrawn in Stage 1, and more in Stage 2. It would benefit businesses that invest in their property, reduce under-use and dereliction of land, increase business profitability and international competitiveness, regenerate deprived areas, have a counter-cyclical impact on the economy, permit infrastructure to become self-funding and reduce tax avoidance and evasion.

The main practical challenge is to find an acceptable way of valuing land separately from the buildings on it. There is little experience of doing so in the UK, and it is widely assumed to be too difficult. However the assessment of land values has been piloted in the UK and implemented in several other jurisdictions. Treasury need to look not just to their usual advisors on valuation (including the Valuation Office Agency, the Royal Institution of Chartered Surveyors and the Institute of Revenues, Rating and Valuation) but to valuers with experience of jurisdictions where LVT is in place and to UK experts such as members of the Professional Land Reform Group.

Land Value Taxation, confined to non-domestic land, could provide a decisive stimulus to business and to economic growth, without increasing the budget deficit. The next step would be for Treasury to carry out a feasibility study.

Glossary

Depreciated Replacement Cost
The replacement cost of a building is the cost of constructing an equivalent replacement (including fees, interest charges and VAT). The Depreciated Replacement Cost is calculated by multiplying this by a depreciation factor that represents both physical and functional obsolescence. The depreciation factor lies in the range from 1 (for a new building as long as it is not already functionally obsolete) to 0 (for a building that would be demolished for the site to be used optimally).

Domestic
'Domestic' means being used wholly for the purposes of living accommodation – including gardens, outhouses, garages and storage premises if these are part of a larger domestic property (Valuation Office Agency 2013a). It is formally defined in section 66(1) of the Local Government Finance Act 1988.

Highest and best use (HABU)
The optimal use (of land) that is legally allowable, physically possible and economically feasible, taking into account any planning conditions and the plans approved by the Local Planning Authority.

Imputed rent
Imputed rent is a term applied to owner-occupied properties, and refers to a notional rent that the owner-as-occupier may be considered to be paying the owner-as-landlord for the use of the land.

Index site
A site that requires valuation.

Land Value Tax (LVT)
A land value tax is a tax equal to a proportion of the market rent of land.

Market rent
The market rent of a plot of land is the 'estimated amount for which a property should lease (let) on the date of valuation between a willing lessor and a willing lessee on appropriate lease terms in an arms-length transaction after proper marketing wherein the parties had each acted knowledgeably, prudently and without compulsion' (RICS 2009:42). 'Market rent' reflects the potential rent achievable from the land when it is put to its highest and best use, and is not necessarily related to the rent that is being paid for its current use. The best method for determining the market rent is direct exposure to the market, which reveals the highest bid that anybody is willing to make.

Market value	The market value (selling price or capital value) of a plot of land is the 'estimated amount for which a property should exchange on the date of valuation between a willing purchaser and a willing vendor in an arms-length transaction after proper marketing wherein the parties had each acted knowledgeably, prudently and without compulsion' (RICS 2009:42).
Marriage value	The additional value that sometimes emerges when two interests in a property are combined or when two adjacent properties are merged. Marriage value results when the value of the whole exceeds the sum of the values of the parts.
Property	Land plus the buildings and other improvements on it.
Sunset clause	A measure within a law or regulation that provides that the law shall cease to have effect after a specific date, unless further legislative action is taken to extend the law.
Yield	Market rent as a percentage of market value.

References

Andelson, Robert (ed) (2000) *Land value taxation around the world* Oxford, Blackwells

AREIS   (Auditors   Real   Estate   Information   System) http://co.lucas.oh.us/index.aspx?NID=377 (accessed 22/10/13)

Ballard Charles L, Shoven John B & Whalley John (1985) *The total welfare cost of the United States tax system: a general equilibrium approach* National Tax Journal *38* 125-140

Barker, Kate (2004) *Delivering stability: securing our future housing needs* London, HMSO

Boles, Nicholas (2011) *It sounds bonkers but we should embrace a land tax* Financial Times (29th September)

Braund, Mark (2010) *Land Value Taxation: a genuine alternative* Guardian (25th September)

Burnham, Andy (2010) *Land Value Taxation – not old or New but true Labour* (Guardian 26th August)

Coalition for Economic Justice (2012) *Land Value Tax: knowledge leads to support* www.landvaluescape.org/archives/2012/12/land-value-tax-knowledge-leads-to-support.html (accessed 8/11/13)

Coalition for Economic Justice (2013) *Reform of Business Rates* www.c4ej.com/cej-publications/reform-of-business-rates (accessed 19/6/13)

Connelan, Owen (2004) *Land Value Taxation in Britain: Experience and opportunities* Cambridge Massachusetts, Lincoln Institute of Land Policy

Department for Transport (2009) *Guidance on value for money* www.dft.gov.uk/about/howthedftworks/vfm/guidanceonvalueformoney (accessed 11/11/13)

Department of the Environment (1988) *Second Interim Evaluation of Enterprise Zones*

Economist (1998) *Unlikely icon* (February 28th)

Economist (2013) *Levying the land: governments should make more use of property taxes* (June 29th)

Elliott, Larry (2010) *Take on the City with a 'people's budget'* 22nd March www.theguardian.com/business/2010/mar/22/budget-2010-rebalancing-economy (accessed 27/8/13)

Emeny, Roger & Wilks, Hector (1984 4th edition) *Principles and practice of rating valuation* London, The Estates Gazette

Feldstein, Martin (1999) *Tax avoidance and the deadweight loss of the Income Tax* Review of Economics and Statistics *81* Issue 4

Froud, Julie; Johal, Sukdev; Law, John; Leaver, Adam and Williams, Karel

(2011) *Rebalancing the economy (or buyer's remorse)* CRESC working paper 87 Milton Keynes, Centre for Research on Socio-Cultural Change

Gauke, David (2014) Letter to Dr Sarah Wollaston MP

Glover, Christopher (2013) *How is land valued?* www.landvaluetax.org/frequently-asked-questions/how-is-land-valued.html (accessed 19/6/13)

GOV.UK (2013 accessed) www.gov.uk/introduction-to-business-rates/overview (accessed 19/6/13)

Graves, Tommas (2011) *Debt is inevitable – unless we change our ways* www.landisfree.co.uk/?p=243 (accessed 22/10/13)

Harberger, Arnold (1964) *Taxation, resource allocation and welfare* in National Bureau of Economic Research and the Brookings Institution

Harrison, Fred (1998) *The losses of nations* London, Othila Press

Hartzog, Alanna (1997) *Pennsylvania's success with local property tax reform: the split rate tax* American Journal of Economics and Sociology (April 1997) reprinted in Hartzog, Alanna (2008)

Hartzog, Alanna (2008) *The earth belongs to everyone* Radford VA, Institute for Economic Democracy

Jackson, Tim (2009/2011) *Prosperity without growth: economics for a finite planet* London, Earthscan

Land Value Tax working party (2005) *The Oxfordshire Land Value Tax Study* Oxford Oxfordshire County Council www.labourland.org/downloads/papers/oxfordshire_land_value_tax_study.pdf (accessed 19/6/13)

LeGrain, Philip (2010) Tax land – it can't be hidden from the Revenue Times (17th June)

McDonnell, John (2007) *Bring in Land Value Tax to replace Council Tax* http://www.johnmcdonnell.org.uk/2007/03/bring-in-land-value-tax-to-replace.html (accessed 22/10/13)

Maxwell, Dominic and Vigor, Anthony (2005) *Time for land tax?* London, IPPR

Mirrlees, James et al (2011) *Tax by design: the Mirrlees Review* London, Institute for Fiscal Studies

Monbiot, George (2013) *Communism, welfare state – what's the next big idea?* Guardian (2nd April)

Muellbaur, John (2005) *Property taxation and the economy* in Dominic Maxwell and Anthony Vigor

National Bureau of Economic Research and the Brookings Institution (1964) *The role of direct and indirect taxes in the Federal Revenue System* Princeton NJ, Princeton University Press

New Zealand Treasury (2005) *Cost benefit analysis primer* www.treasury.govt.nz/publications/guidance/planning/costbenefitanalysis/ primer/cba-primer-v12.pdf (accessed 26th August 2013)

Norregaard, John (2013) *Taxing immovable property: revenue potential and implementation challenges* IMF Working Paper WP/13/129, May 2013

OECD (2010) *Tax policy reform and economic growth* Paris OECD tax policy studies No 20

Plimmer, Frances (1998) *Rating law and valuation: a practical guide* London, Addison Wesley Longman

Pratt, Julian (2011) *Stewardship economy: private property without private ownership* Lulu www.stewardship.ac

Ramsey, Frank (1927) *A contribution to the theory of taxation* Economic Journal 47-61

RICS (2009) *RICS Valuation standards (Red book)* London Royal Institution of Chartered Surveyors

Sully, Rob (2011) *Schools business rates policy is labelled perverse* Carmarthern Journal 3/8/11 www.thisissouthwales.co.uk/Schools-business-rates-policy-labelled-perverse/story-13060530-detail/story.html#ixzz2VyZXInaz (accessed 19/6/13)

Toynbee, Polly (2009) www.theguardian.com/commentisfree/2009/sep/07/labour-radical-ideas-electoral-reform (accessed 27/8/13)

Trades Union Congress (TUC) (2011) Conference Decisions 2011, Alternative Economic Strategy www.tuc.org.uk/the_tuc/tuc-20074-f0.cfm (accessed 19/6/13)

Valuation Office Agency (2013a) www.voa.gov.uk/corporate/Publications/Manuals/RatingManual/RatingManualVolume4/sect2/b-rat-man-vol4-s2-partb-dom.html#P91_2460 (accessed 19/6/13)

Valuation Office Agency (2013b) www.voa.gov.uk/corporate/Publications/Manuals/RatingManual/RatingManualVolume4/sect1/rat-man-vol4-s1.htm (accessed 19/6/13)

Valuation Office Agency (2010) www.2010.voa.gov.uk/rli/static/HelpPages/English/faqs/faq116-what_does_rv_mean.html (accessed 19/6/13)

Vickrey, William (1995) *Simplification, progression and a level playing field* reprinted in Wenzer, Kenneth (1999:17)

Vickers, Tony (2007) *Location matters: recycling Britain's wealth* London Shepheard-Walwyn

Vickers, Tony (2009) *Visualising landvaluescape: developing the case for Britain* Kingston upon Thames, PhD Thesis

Wadsworth, Mark (2013) http://markwadsworth.blogspot.co.uk/ (accessed 27/8/13)

Wenzer, Kenneth (1999) *Land Value Taxation: the equitable and efficient source of public finance* London, Shepheard-Walwyn

Wetzel, Dave (2013) *Land Value Tax with residential exemptions* (unpublished – personal communication)

Wilks, Hector (1964) *Rating of site values: report of a pilot survey at Whitstable* London, Rating and Valuing Association www.landvaluetax.org/frequently-asked-questions/how-is-land-valued.html (accessed 19/6/13)

Wilks, Hector (1974) *Site Value Rating: report on a research carried out in the town of Whitstable* London, The Land Institute www.landvaluetax.org/frequently-asked-questions/how-is-land-valued.html (accessed 19/6/13)

Wolf, Martin (2010) *Why we must halt the land cycle* Financial Times July 8th 2010

⊛ creative commons

Creative Commons is a not-for-profit organization

It works to increase the amount of creativity (cultural, educational, and scientific) in the 'cultural commons' — the body of work that is available to the public for free and legal sharing and use.

CC provides free, easy-to-use legal tools

Creative Commons gives everyone from individual creators to large companies and institutions a simple, standardised way to grant permissions to their creative work. The Creative Commons licences define the spectrum of possibilities between full copyright protection (*all* rights reserved) and the public domain (*no* rights reserved).

Some Rights Reserved

The licenses enable the creator to retain copyright while allowing certain specified uses — a 'some rights reserved' copyright.

CC Licenses work alongside copyright

Creative Commons licenses are not an alternative to copyright. They work alongside copyright, so a creator can modify the copyright terms to best suit their needs.

About the Henry George Society of Devon

Initiated in 2012, the Henry George Society of Devon is an informal group with a shared enthusiasm for the ideas of 19th century political economist Henry George. His central proposal is that all taxes should be removed and replaced by a charge for the use of land – the Single Tax or Land Value Tax. We feel that this is essential if prosperity is to be shared by all in society.

Therefore our stated aim is to foster and promote a greater understanding of Georgist economics in Devon UK. We do this by "flying the Georgist flag" and providing a point of contact, forum and support network for likeminded people in this part of the world. We also give presentations, host discussions and provide information to individuals and groups.

We believe that correctly understanding the fundamental root cause of the problem is the most vital step towards solving it. Our activities are therefore first and foremost directed at education. As George himself wrote:

> "Until there be correct thought, there cannot be right action, and when there is correct thought, right action will follow" (Social Problems, 1886).

Individual members undertake a variety of activities such as speaking engagements, writing books, hooking up with other groups and speaking to politicians. Our meetings, held four or five times each year, are an opportunity to share experiences, listen to guest speakers and discuss the issues of the day. These meetings are always open to newcomers who are curious to learn more. If you would like to learn about Georgist economics, would like us to give a talk or wish to join us and/or help us further our aims please get in touch by emailing henrygeorgedevon@gmail.com.

Also published by the Henry George Society of Devon:

Jonty Williams (2014) Husbandry: an ancient art for the modern world

http://henrygeorgedevon.wordpress.com